MY GRANDMOTHER'S
CHINESE KITCHEN

MY GRANDMOTHER'S CHINESE KITCHEN

100 FAMILY RECIPES AND LIFE LESSONS

EILEEN YIN-FEI LO

BRUSH CALLIGRAPHY BY SAN YAN WONG

HOME

A HOME BOOK
Published by the Penguin Group
Penguin Group (USA) Inc.
375 Hudson Street, New York, New York 10014, USA
Penguin Group (Canada), 90 Eglinton Avenue East, Suite 700, Toronto, Ontario M4P 2Y3, Canada
(a division of Pearson Penguin Canada Inc.)
Penguin Books Ltd., 80 Strand, London WC2R 0RL, England
Penguin Group Ireland, 25 St. Stephen's Green, Dublin 2, Ireland (a division of Penguin Books Ltd.)
Penguin Group (Australia), 250 Camberwell Road, Camberwell, Victoria 3124, Australia
(a division of Pearson Australia Group Pty. Ltd.)
Penguin Books India Pvt. Ltd., 11 Community Centre, Panchsheel Park, New Delhi—110 017, India
Penguin Group (NZ), Cnr. Airborne and Rosedale Roads, Albany, Auckland 1310, New Zealand
(a division of Pearson New Zealand Ltd.)
Penguin Books (South Africa) (Pty.) Ltd., 24 Sturdee Avenue, Rosebank, Johannesburg 2196, South Africa

Penguin Books Ltd., Registered Offices: 80 Strand, London WC2R 0RL, England

While the author has made every effort to provide accurate telephone numbers and Internet addresses at the time of publication, neither the publisher nor the author assumes any responsibility for errors, or for changes that occur after publication. Further, the publisher does not have any control over and does not assume any responsibility for author or third-party websites or their content.

MY GRANDMOTHER'S CHINESE KITCHEN

First edition: December 2006

Home hardcover ISBN: 1-55788-505-2

An application to register this book for cataloging has been submitted to the Library of Congress.

PRINTED IN THE UNITED STATES OF AMERICA

10 9 8 7 6 5 4 3 2 1

PUBLISHER'S NOTE: The recipes contained in this book are to be followed exactly as written. The publisher is not responsible for your specific health or allergy needs that may require medical supervision. The publisher is not responsible for any adverse reactions to the recipes contained in this book.

Most Home Books are available at special quantity discounts for bulk purchases for sales promotions, premiums, fund-raising, or educational use. Special books, or book excerpts, can also be created to fit specific needs. For details, write: Special Markets, The Berkley Publishing Group, 375 Hudson Street, New York, New York 10014.

This book is, as always, for those I love, and upon whose counsel and taste I rely:
my husband, Fred, and my children, Christopher, Elena and Stephen.
To this small family I add, with joy, my granddaughter, Elliott Antonia,
to whom I have given the name Siu Fung, or Little Phoenix,
and whom I call Siu Siu. A special thanks belongs to
Carla Glasser, my agent, who works very hard
on my behalf. Very hard.

CONTENTS

MY GRANDMOTHER

NOW THAT I AM A GRANDMOTHER, I realize how important it is that I impart some of my experiences to my granddaughter, Siu Siu. Her mother will, as did my mother, give her most of her basic lessons in life. Reserved for me will be two pleasures: first simply enjoying and loving her, and second, seeing to it that my granddaughter learns and keeps whole many aspects of her ancestral, partially Chinese, culture and, quite important to me, her culinary heritage. It was what my grandmother, my Ah Paw, gave to me when I was a girl in China, in those many, many times I visited her and her kitchen. I learned manners and discipline, aspects of proper behavior that I adhere to today, patience and traditional tested ways of doing things. Not only did she teach me to cook practically, but saw to it that I learned as well the methods and philosophies of cookery, the joy of creation. She inculcated in me the truth that cooking well for someone is giving love in a most tangible way. The dishes I learned from my grandmother I cook to this day, very much in her way, her classics, her tradition. I am her heirloom. These my granddaughter will learn, as she grows.

Allow me to share my Ah Paw with you.

My maternal grandmother, my Ah Paw, was a most unusual and wondrous woman. When I was growing up in the Guangdong district of Sun Tak, I would not mind walking the more than two hours it took to go from my village to hers because I wanted to be with her as much as I was able. I spent most of my holidays from school as well as many weekends with her, and much of my extended school vacation time, with the blessings of my mother, Lo Chan Miu Hau, her daughter.

Her formal title was Loi Joh Moh, or grandmother of my mother's side of our family, and she had been our matriarch since the death of her husband, Ah Gung, in the Sino-Japanese War. In fact, because he had been so actively anti-Japanese, all traces of him in our family had been burned—photographs, letters, clothing, official documents of his standing as a municipal mandarin. These were followed by similar burning of all family records so as not to provide information that might be used by the Japanese invaders, which explains why few pictures of my family exist, and none of my Ah Paw.

The words *Ah Paw* are actually a diminutive, quite like *Grandma* in English. She was a small woman, very thin, and weighed only about seventy pounds. Her feet had been bound as a baby and were only three inches long, always encased in tiny black silk slippers over white socks, a vivid vestige of that almost feudal custom wherein women's feet were bound to demonstrate not only that they were high-born but were so well off that it was never necessary for them to need to walk, that everything would be done for them. Bound feet were symbols of a life of ease for Ah Paw, who never walked more than a few steps, the shortest of distances, in all the years I was with her. She was helped by her servants, occasionally by me. For her meals, a table was brought to her and whatever family attended sat arrayed around her. She was not, in fact, pleased that my mother, when she was a little girl of ten, tore off her own foot bindings and refused thereafter to have her feet bound.

She only wore black *sam fu*, those loose blouse-and-trouser combinations, had her black, gray-streaked hair pulled back and wound into a bun. In the colder winter months she wore a wide black silk headband embroidered with pearls and jade. The only other jewelry or ornamentation I ever saw her wear were golden hoops in her pierced ears. She spent all of her days in her combined living room and parlor. Her servants Sau Lin, or "Beautiful Lotus," and Ah Guk, "Chrysanthemum," would support her if she needed to go any significant distance, such as a walk to her vegetable garden.

Otherwise she tottered by herself from her bedroom to her living room each day. Occasionally I would provide support for her as we walked into her open plaza so she could sit in the sun and talk with her friends, women only. She was quite independent despite her inability to walk properly.

She was aristocratic, spoke softly, never raised her voice in anger that I can remember and was looked upon within the family as a final arbiter. She was an autocrat as well and called Yee Dai Yun by outsiders, which translated loosely as the revered first wife of the second son of my great-grandfather. Within our family she was referred to by her relationships to individual daughters, nieces, cousins and so on. I never knew her name. She was always only, Ah Paw.

Ah Paw was steeped in the religion of Buddha and the manners and behavior of Confucius. She burned incense throughout her days to the heavenly gods, whom she hoped looked after her family members both dead and alive. She passed her prayer beads through her fingers very often each day, praying for her late husband and son, and the two grandsons who had died as infants. When she spoke it was with softness, very softly, and she taught, with traditional adages and aphorisms—most of which, as it turned out, was about food and its consumption—to illustrate her teachings. She called me Ah Fei, which to me was an endearment; to her it was a pet name that she said indicated I was intelligent and could fly. I wanted to be with her, just to sit on the floor next to her divan as she talked about proper, traditional ways of doing things, how things were, as they should be, in her world. I loved staying with her at her house because I would sleep with her in her big, intricately carved red-lacquered bed, the bed that had been part of her marriage dowry.

Speak quietly and softly, she would caution me, *bun hau tak yan jung,* which meant that if you spoke badly of people, all others would never like you.

"Bun leg tak wun moon dum dum," she would say, as I listened, suggesting that if I used my energy to help someone, to do a favor, I would be rewarded with a bowl of rice or sweets.

Do not be a *fan tong,* she would caution, which meant that I should not sit and do nothing in the manner of a *fan tong*: a rice bucket, which cannot move. Rather, I should be active.

In tandem with this she would tell me not to be a *bun tong soi,* a half-filled bucket of water. Instead, I should finish whatever task I was given, even to the extent of doing it repeatedly until it was done right.

Nor should I be a *dai dun op*: a big lazy duck too stupid to learn.

I do not doubt for a moment that it was Ah Paw who taught the big black mynah bird that perched in her parlor to say, *"Ah Mui. Ah Mui, mo hah sik, toh sahn seng,"* in which the mynah would call to my cousin saying, "I don't have shrimp to eat, my stomach is getting rusty," which was an automatic signal for my cousin and me to run to a nearby river and catch a sufficient number of live shrimp to satisfy her mynah. The mynah was gone upon one visit when I was about seven years old. Ah Paw told me later that he had died and was with my grandfather in heaven. But the mynah's message about doing something instead of nothing was never lost upon me.

Ah Paw took it upon herself to teach me to cook, and to do this one should begin at the beginning: how to steam fish to the precise state of doneness, and to finish it with boiled peanut oil. I learned first to clean a fish and remove its scales, gills, intestines and membranes, then to wash it thoroughly before letting it rest. Then I salted and peppered it under the watchful eyes of the servants, seasoned it with soy sauce, a bit of peanut oil, ginger, scallions and coriander sprigs. I can still recall the first fish I prepared. I was most proud of myself, and brought the fish to my grandmother who looked at it, smelled it and said, quietly, *"Ng gei dok lok sohk yau,"* which translates as "You forgot the boiled oil, take it back to the kitchen and pour the oil." I never forgot again.

She suggested to me that vegetables should be chosen with at least the same care given to selecting in-laws, and that no vegetable should be eaten if it had been out of the ground for more than two hours. She warned me that for every uneaten rice kernel I left in my rice bowl my future husband would have a pock on his face. Meats were to be cut into perfectly matching lengths and widths as Confucius had directed. Furthermore I should never shout in the kitchen, nor berate servants, who to Ah Paw were less servants than they were constant attending members of her family. Such unseemly kitchen conduct would be reported by our Kitchen God, Tsao Chun, to the gods in heaven and would reflect badly upon our family.

Ah Paw taught me to cook because my mother could not, completely, and because my father, Lo Pak Wan, who was a fine cook, was away from our home for great lengths of time. My mother had come to my father's house in marriage with a dowry that included three servants. She cooked but rarely, because that was part of the servants' work. The war years in China, however, led to upheaval. Servants left, were married, or both, and my mother found herself without her servants, without anyone to cook for her. She had to learn, and my initial forays into the kitchen were with her, both of us discovering as we went. Out of this experience came my mother's belief that I should learn to cook as early, and as well, as possible.

My father, when I was a baby, was away for years seeking the golden mountain as far away as South Africa. Later he was an adviser to my uncle, who was described in our family as a senator-soldier initially in Canton, then later elsewhere in war-ravaged China. This kept my father away from our family for much of my girlhood. It remained for my older brother, Ching Moh, to become my substitute father for such things as school attendance and permissions. Thus it was this combination of circumstances as well as Ah Paw's love for me, and my desire to be with her that led my grandmother to see to my cooking education through stories and practice.

Ah Paw knew instinctively, I believe, how things ought to be done without ever having put a spatula into a wok, without ever setting a bamboo steamer over boiling water, without ever having set foot in a kitchen. She knew which foods wedded, which clashed. She was a brilliant kitchen chemist with an encyclopedic knowledge of foods. She would tell the servants what foods to buy at the market, what to pick from her vast gardens and orchards, what fish to fetch and then instruct them with fine precision how to cook them, and for how long. She was never wrong, that I can remember, and she amazed me with her knowledge, which she continually transmitted to me. She made certain, despite the presence of her servants, that every visit to her house, whether on school holiday or at family festival involved me being in her kitchen.

I would listen wide-eyed, all ears, as she imparted kitchen practices. Most of what I know about food, its meaning, its truth, its preparation has come from her. I truly believe that my palate is my inheritance from her. This culinary education came from the time I was four through the last years of the Chinese-Japanese Wars and into the beginnings of revolutionary China when I fled China for Hong Kong before my twelfth birthday. Ah Paw was more than sixty-five years old then. To this day my various cousins tell me that as I have grown older I have come to look more and more like my Ah Paw. This pleases me.

On the pages that follow, I will share my Ah Paw's wisdom and some of the recipes she taught me—the ones I treasure the most.

ONE

MY GRANDMOTHER,
MY TEACHER

THE PATH TO MY GRANDMOTHER'S HOUSE wound through waving fronds of sugarcane, groves of mulberry bushes being grown for silkworms to eat and rice fields, a meandering way from our village of Siu Lo Chun to her larger town of Sah Gau. Both lay within Sun Tak Yeun, or the Sun Tak District, an important wedge of Guangdong Province, between Guangzhou, or Canton, of which it was a suburb, and Macau to the south.

It was a pleasant journey of more than two hours through this greenery, and my mother and I used to enjoy the serenity away from the main road. When I was a very little girl walking with my mother, however, our peace was occasionally marred by vestiges of the Chinese-Japanese War, wrecked carts and military trucks, even a stray

MY MOTHER, LO CHUN MIU HAU.

dead soldier. These were the remains of the retreating defeated Japanese army. When we spotted such horrifying sights, my mother would tell me to shield my eyes and run ahead until I could see nothing but plantings, which I did.

These I recall with vivid clarity, but by the war's end, when I was about eight years old, I was able to go to my grandmother's house alone, the walk sweet with anticipation, the arrival even sweeter because my Ah Paw was always there to welcome me with, "*Ah Fei*, I have been waiting for you."

My grandmother's house, brick, two stories tall, with its own small plaza, was the center of her small but nevertheless significant empire, which consisted of four houses that provided shelter for relatives and servants, a vast plot of several acres planted with vegetables and fruit tree orchards, a stretch of fish-bearing river and several large man-made freshwater ponds (really more small lakes than ponds), in which different varieties of carp were farmed. It is no wonder that among the many shrines to the gods that stood about her house, one of high prominence was the paper image of Shen Nung, the God of Agriculture, who it is said wrote the first book ever concerning food, a compendium of hundreds of herbs.

The core of her house was its kitchen, watched over by the paper image of its own god Tsao Chun, the God of the Hearth, whose function it was before each New Year to tell the gods above only good things about our family after we had smeared the lips of his picture with honey and then burned it to send him skyward.

On the ground floor of Ah Paw's were five rooms, all off a wide entry watched over by three gods: the God of Entrances, Wei Chung; and the Door Gods, Shen Shu to the left and Yu Lei on the right—all there to keep evil or mischievous spirits from entering the house. All of the house's first-floor rooms were off a center hall. My grandmother's bedroom was first, off to the left, with a door connecting to a room that was Ah Paw's salon, living room and dining room, dominated by her divan where she spent most of her days, and where we ate our meals. It also was the home of a shrine to my grandmother's ancestors and to Guan Gung, the God of Fairness and Justice. This room in turn connected to another bedroom at the rear of the house. When I was small, I slept with Ah Paw in the front bedroom; when I grew older the rear bedroom was reserved for me.

To the right side of the long hall was a large room used to store clothing and furniture, and in the rear of the house was the large, always fragrant kitchen. Between the store rooms and kitchen was an open terrace, which Ah Paw called the room open to the heavens. The second floor of the house was devoted to a very long windowless room, where various dried and preserved foods were stored and where her servants slept, and to two tiled terraces overlooking the open space below. There was a hole, surrounded by a railing, in the floor of this great room, just above my grandmother's ancestor, so that the altar would be respected and no one would walk on it.

The most important room of the house, to be sure, was the kitchen, quite large and filled with wonder. It contained five cooking stoves, all constructed of brick, with ceramic tile tops. One, to the right, was huge with a large round hole in its top, used for the largest of my grandmother's iron woks. In front, on the side of the stove was another hole into which the firewood was fed to fuel the cooking fire. On the other side of the kitchen was a long stove, at least six feet in length, as I can recall. The four round holes in its top were of different sizes to accommodate woks and clay pots of different sizes. It also had four additional holes for adding wood to its fires. An enormous amount of food, as you can imagine, could be cooked in this kitchen. As in most of the rest of domestic China at that time, there were no home ovens. We could not roast or barbecue large slabs of pork or whole pigs. Nor could we roast ducks, geese or chickens. We were able to smoke, steam and long cook in woks, or stew in clay pots, but these were always on top of the stoves. We could, however, do small barbecues and roasts, such as loins of pork, on a small ceramic, charcoal-fed burner, which Ah Paw kept in an open area just outside of the kitchen door.

At the far end of this four-hole stove was a large wood cabinet, which held bowls, cups, serving dishes and platters, and steamers, spatulas and ladles, and beside this cabinet was a wall board. Attached was a long peg, on which hung the various covers for the woks. Beside the entrance to the kitchen, inside from that open area was a very big clay jar, which held fresh water, and on the wall above it was a holder for all of the family's chopsticks. Next to the water jar stood a high pile of cut firewood that was continually replenished. On the other side of the entry to the kitchen was a large wood preparation table.

All of this comprised Ah Paw's *chi fong*, literally her "kitchen room," where, at my grandmother's behest, my first cooking lesson was given to me by her servants Sau Lin and Ah Guk.

I was to learn to cook rice. Nothing was more important than rice, Ah Paw told me that morning, *"Yut lop mai dai guor tin,"* which means, "One grain of rice is bigger than the sky," and implies that the sky, no matter how vast, could not feed one's hunger, yet rice could. Rice was the center of most of our meals, with seafood, vegetables and meats arrayed around it. In our conversations, if a person was well off his rice bowl was said to be full; if poor, his bowl was said to be empty. It was important, my grandmother said, to learn to prepare rice perfectly.

Nor should this be troublesome. It has been said often, and incorrectly, that making fluffy cooked rice, with separated grains, is difficult. This is not so; it is, in fact, easy. Here is the recipe I learned in my grandmother's kitchen decades ago. I make it exactly the same way today. Uncooked rice is called *mai*; after cooking it is called *fan*. This is perfect fan.

Perfect Cooked Rice

(FAN)

2 cups extra-long-grain rice (rices grown in the southern United States and jasmine rice from Thailand are preferred)

15 ounces cold water

Place rice in a pot with sufficient water to cover. Wash rice three times in the cold water in the pot by rubbing it between your hands. Drain well after washing. Add 15 ounces water to the rice and allow it to rest for 1 hour before cooking. I prefer that so-called old rice be used—rice that has been lying about in sacks for extended periods, for it will absorb water better and will cook easier. (It is often suggested that a ratio of 2 cups of rice to 2 cups of water be used. This is unsatisfactory because it will be too soft.)

Begin cooking the rice, uncovered, over high heat, by bringing the water to a boil. Stir the rice with a wooden spoon or chopsticks and cook about 4 minutes or until the water is absorbed, or evaporates. Even after the water is gone, the rice will continue to be quite hard. Cover the pot and cook over very low heat for about 8 minutes more, stirring the rice from time to time.

Turn off the heat and loosen the rice with the wooden spoon or chopsticks. This will help it retain its fluffiness. Cover tightly until ready to serve. Just before serving, stir and loosen the rice once again. Well-cooked rice will have absorbed the water but will not be lumpy, nor will the kernels stick together. They will be firm and separate. The rice may be kept hot in a warm oven for an hour without drying out.

MAKES 4½ TO 5 CUPS OF RICE

N O T E The older the rice the higher the yield. This is the rice I refer to throughout this book when I suggest eating dishes with cooked rice.

STOCKS

Just as rice was a kitchen necessity, so were stocks, upon which virtually all good recipes depend. My grandmother's cooks regularly made stocks from chickens and their parts, and from vegetables. Since there was no refrigeration in these parts of rural China, these stocks would last, and be used, within days. These days, they will keep, refrigerated, for four to five days, and may be frozen for up to three months. These stock recipes may be cut in half.

Chicken Stock

(GAI SEUNG TONG)

1 gallon water

3 pounds chicken wings

2 whole chickens (8 pounds) including giblets, fat removed, each chicken cut into 4 pieces

2 gallons cold water

½ pound fresh ginger, cut into 3 pieces, lightly smashed

6 garlic cloves, peeled

2 bunches scallions, trimmed, cut into thirds

4 medium onions, peeled and quartered

¼ pound (1 cup) fresh coriander, cut into thirds

½ cup fried onions (page 16)

¼ cup boxthorn seeds, soaked 10 minutes

3 to 4 tablespoons salt, to taste

In a large stockpot, bring 1 gallon of water to a boil. Add chicken, chicken wings and giblets, return to a boil for 1 minute. (This will bring the blood and juices to the top of the liquid.) Turn off heat. Pour off water and run cold water into the pot to rinse chicken. Drain.

Place chicken, chicken wings, and giblets back in pot. Add 2 gallons of cold water and all remaining ingredients except salt. Cover pot and bring to a boil over high heat. Reduce heat to a simmer, leaving lid open a crack. Simmer for 4½ hours. Stir stock from time to time, skimming off residue from the surface. Stir in salt about 30 minutes before end of cooking time. (The addition of salt is for preservation as well as for taste. The amount used depends, of course, upon individual taste.)

Turn off heat. Allow to cool for 10 to 15 minutes. Strain and pour into containers to store for later use.

YIELDS ABOUT 5 QUARTS

NOTE Boxthorn seeds (see page 247) come in ½-pound to 1-pound packages. After opening, store in a covered glass jar. They will keep for at least 6 months. There is no substitute for boxthorn seeds in this recipe. They provide some flavor and have health properties, the Chinese believe. If unavailable, make recipe without.

Vegetable Stock

(Jai Seung Tong)

5 quarts cold water

1 pound carrots, peeled, cut into thirds

2 bunches scallions, trimmed, cut into thirds

3 pounds onions, quartered

1 pound fresh mushrooms, cut into thirds

8 stalks celery, halved

¼ pound (1 cup) fresh coriander, cut into thirds

½ cup Chinese preserved dates (or preserved figs), soaked in hot water 30 minutes, washed

¼ cup boxthorn seeds, soaked in hot water 10 minutes, washed (or 6 pitted sweet dates)

¼ pound fresh ginger, left in piece, lightly smashed

½ cup fried scallions (page 16)

2 to 3 tablespoons salt, to taste

Bring water to a boil in a large pot. Add all ingredients except salt. Reduce heat and simmer at a slow boil in a partially covered pot for 4 hours. Stir occasionally during simmering, skim if necessary. Stir in salt, return to a boil, reduce heat immediately, simmer for 20 minutes.

Turn off heat. When stock is cooled, remove from heat, strain. Discard solids. Store stock in containers until needed. The recipe may be cut in half.

MAKES 3½ TO 4 QUARTS STOCK

NOTE Preserved dates can be found in Asian groceries and come in 1-pound plastic packages labeled either "red dates" or "dates." After opening the package, the dates should be placed in a covered glass jar and stored in a cool place. They will keep six months.

In this recipe, customary sweet dates, usually from the Middle East, may be used if boxthorn seeds are unavailable. The dates provide some color and sweetness, and enrich the stock.

OILS

Because there was no refrigeration in my grandmother's kitchen, infused oils were made on almost a daily basis. Ah Paw preferred it that way. The oils below can be kept for a week at room temperature, or for as long as three months if refrigerated. They also provide a bonus, because you can use the fried onions as an ingredient in the Chicken Stock, and fried scallions in the Vegetable Stock.

Scallion Oil

(CHUNG YAU)

1½ cups peanut oil

3 to 4 bunches of scallions (1 pound), well dried, trimmed, each scallion cut into 2-inch pieces, white portions lightly smashed

Heat wok over high heat for 30 seconds. Add oil and scallions, stir and mix well, make certain scallions are immersed in oil. Bring to a boil. Lower the heat, and simmer the oil and scallions for 20 minutes, stirring occasionally, until scallions brown. Turn off heat, strain oil through a fine strainer into a bowl and cool to room temperature. Pour into a glass jar, cover and refrigerate until needed.

MAKES 1 ¼ CUPS

Onion Oil

(YUNG CHUNG YAU)

1½ cups peanut oil

1 pound (4 cups) yellow onions, very thinly sliced

Heat wok over high heat for 30 seconds. Add peanut oil, then onions. Stir, making certain onions are coated. Cook for 7 minutes, stirring and turning often to prevent burning. Lower heat to medium and cook for 15 minutes more, or until onions turn light brown. Strain oil into a bowl, using a spoon or a ladle to press onions as they drain. Allow to cool. Pour into a glass jar, cover and refrigerate until needed.

MAKES 1 ¼ CUPS

ANOTHER OF THE SIGNIFICANT FOODS THAT came from my grandmother's kitchen was preserved salted pork, which, like the preceding stocks and oils, was a food of necessity and versatility, its preparation the result of the lack of refrigeration. In the traditional large Chinese larder meat is pork. When we say "meat" we mean pork. Historically there was lamb and mutton, as well as occasionally beef, in the north and west of China, but for most of the country, even to this day, when the subject is meat, the meaning is pork. It was preserved pork, alone or in combination with other foods and rice, that warmed us in winter, and in many smaller villages like mine, pigs were slaughtered annually and their meat distributed.

In my village of Siu Lo Chun this annual rite was called *Tai Gung Fun Ji Yuk*, which translates as "ancestor-distributed pork." Land, considered community property, was administered by community officials, of which my father was one. Before each Lunar New Year the farming lands were leased to farmers who bid. The money from these bids was used to buy pigs, which were slaughtered, their meat cut up and boiled and then distributed. The distribution seems somewhat unfair since it was allotted only to the male members of the village families. The more males, the more pork. My family actually benefited from the practice, because with my father, brother, quite a few uncles and male cousins, we received quite a lot of pork. Once the pork had been given out it would be placed in crocks, heavily salted, and left to cure for at least a month, insuring that we would have ample pork to last us through the winter.

This custom did not exist in Ah Paw's town of Sah Gau. It was less a community village than mine and there, pork was simply purchased from butchers and then salted in the traditional way. Usually, the pork to be salted was slabs of fresh belly meat, bacon, which consisted of a good deal of fat and skin. My version utilizes a good-sized pork loin, though I cure it exactly as it was done in my grandmother's kitchen.

The salted pork was used in many ways. It was eaten in rice congees. It was steamed with fish and stir-fried with various vegetables. We made soups with it. My grandmother even steamed the salted pork with fresh pork.

Salted Pork

(HAM JI YUK)

咸猪肉

4 pounds boneless pork loin

2 quarts cold water, or enough to cover pork

1 slice fresh ginger, 1 inch thick, lightly smashed

4 cloves garlic, peeled

6 scallions, white portions only

3½ tablespoons salt

Place all ingredients, except salt, in a large pot. Cover and bring to a boil over high heat. Reduce heat, leave lid slightly open and simmer 45 minutes to 1 hour. Turn the pork halfway through simmer. Turn off heat. Remove pork from pot and place in a large bowl of ice water; allow pork loin to rest 5 minutes until it cools.

Remove pork from water. Place in a shallow dish and sprinkle salt over top, rubbing it well into the pork. Cover the pork and allow it to refrigerate untouched for 1 day. It is now ready for use. The salted pork will keep refrigerated for at least a week.

In China, as I have noted, the heavy salting permitted us to keep the pork for at least a month. It should not be frozen because its fiber will soften and defrosting will cause the salting to run off.

LEFTOVER RICE WAS A FAVORITE OF Ah Paw's and mine as well, and was the rice eaten most often in her house. I make it to this day for my family and my granddaughter, Siu Siu. It is easy to make, is delicious and as a practical matter, illustrates the felicitous combining of all of the preceding basic recipes. The name for this leftover rice is *chau lahng fan*, which translates literally as "cold rice stir-fried." There was always rice at Ah Paw's table, and it was her explicit instruction that at lunch extra rice should be cooked so that we would have enough to make this special rice at dinner.

Leftover Rice

(Chau Lahng Fan)

3½ tablespoons Scallion Oil (page 16)

4 jumbo eggs, lightly beaten with ¼ teaspoon salt and 1 tablespoon Chicken Stock (page 13)

2 teaspoons minced ginger

1 cup onions, cut into ¼-inch dice

1½ cups Salted Pork (page 18), cut into ⅓-inch dice

5 cups cooked rice

3 scallions, thinly sliced across

Heat wok over high heat for 30 seconds. Add 1½ tablespoons oil, coat wok with spatula. When a wisp of white smoke appears, add beaten egg and scramble until firm. Remove, cut up coarsely and reserve.

Wipe wok and spatula with paper towels to remove egg residue. Reheat over high heat and add remaining oil to coat wok. Add ginger and stir. Add onions, stir and cook 2 minutes until onions soften. Add pork, stir to mix well, cook for 2 minutes more. Add rice. Stir to mix all ingredients thoroughly. Cook 4 to 5 minutes, until mixture is very hot. If rice is dry and begins to stick to wok, add an additional tablespoon of oil. Add reserved eggs, mix and cook for 2 minutes more. Add ¼ to ½ teaspoon salt, if necessary, to taste. Mix well. Add scallions, turn off heat and toss until mixed. Serve immediately.

MAKES 4 TO 6 SERVINGS

ALMOST EVERY MORNING AT AH PAW'S house we ate congee, a rice soup made from two kinds of rice: glutinous, so-called sweet rice, and short-grained rice, identical to that used by Japanese sushi chefs. The Chinese believe congee is a dish that's a thousand years old. The soup, closer to a porridge, consisted of small amounts of rice, larger amounts of water, and was, and is, considered to be a morning restorative, easily digestible and nourishing to infants as well as to the aged. I can tell you that my granddaughter loves her morning congee. It is said to reduce the body's heat, and was the only food eaten when one was feverish.

Congee is one of those Chinese dishes with a long lineage. Where we lived in southern China, it was, and still is, made with two rices. In other parts of the country it has been made from wheat, barley, sorghum, millet, tapioca, even corn, occasionally in combination with rice, though most often without. Over the years it has been flavored with chrysanthemums, pears, ginseng, ginger, lotus root and mint.

Though primarily a breakfast preparation it is often eaten at lunch as well, and occasionally for dinner. It is most adaptable and welcomes such additions as meats, vegetables, preserved eggs, fish and seafood, even a Chinese version of black pudding made from pork blood, which make a more elaborate soup, suitable even for the evening meal or a late snack.

There is a familiar folktale concerning congee, which relates to its Chinese name, *jook*. It is said that a miserly man invited guests to his house for dinner and instructed his cook, whose name was Ah Fook, to stretch his cooked rice by ladling water into it. The signal to so dilute would be when the man called the cook's name. During the day, however, as the cook was preparing the rice and other dishes, the man would call him on other matters, yet each time the cook heard his name, Ah Fook, he would add a ladle of water to the rice, so that by dinnertime what remained was not cooked rice but the thinnest of congees.

The cook was so upset, he berated his master with *"Ah Fook, Ah Fook, Ah Fook. Fook mut yeh, bin jor wok jook,"* the loose translation of which is "You have called my name so often that my wok of rice has become a wok of congee."

I loved to hear Ah Paw tell me this story, even though I had heard it many times, because it made me laugh so hard, even as she was teaching me to be generous, particularly with sharing food.

Congee

(JOOK)

½ cup short-grain rice

⅓ cup glutinous rice

8½ cups cold water

Salt, to taste

Place rices in a large pot. Wash three times under water by rubbing the kernels between your hands. Drain.

Return rice to pot, add 8½ cups cold water, cover and bring to a boil over high heat. Leave the pot lid slightly open, reduce heat to medium-low and cook for 1 hour, stirring often to prevent the rice from sticking to the bottom of the pot. Cook until the rice thickens almost to the consistency of porridge. Add salt to taste, stir. Remove from heat and serve.

MAKES 4 TO 6 SERVINGS

Congee with Fish

(YUE JOOK)

1 recipe Congee (page 22)

1 whole 3-pound fresh fish (Grass carp was usually Ah Paw's fish of choice; however, striped bass or sea bass may be used. A 3-pound fresh fish will yield 1½ pounds, skinned and boned.)

MARINADE

2 teaspoons Chinese white rice vinegar or distilled white vinegar

2 tablespoons Chinese white rice wine, or gin

3 teaspoons light soy sauce

2 teaspoons sesame oil

2 tablespoons peanut oil

1 teaspoon salt

Pinch white pepper

4 slices fresh ginger, sliced paper thin, julienned

2 scallions, trimmed, cut into 1½-inch pieces

1 tablespoon Scallion Oil (page 16)

⅛ teaspoon white pepper

1 teaspoon light soy sauce

3 scallions, trimmed, finely sliced, for garnish

1 tablespoon fresh coriander, finely sliced, for garnish (optional)

While the congee is cooking, place the fish in a heatproof dish. Combine the marinade ingredients well and pour over fish. Place ginger and scallions from the marinade beneath the fish, in its cavity, and on top. Steam the fish for 25 minutes. (See steaming directions, page 30.)

Remove fish from steamer and allow to cool to room temperature. Discard the skin, bones, ginger and scallions and break the fish flesh into small pieces. Place fish in a bowl, add Scallion Oil, white pepper and soy sauce and mix lightly with fish. When congee is cooked add the fish to it, mix well and allow congee to come to a boil. Turn off heat, pour congee into a heated tureen, sprinkle the scallions on top, and coriander, if desired. Serve immediately.

MAKES 6 SERVINGS

N O T E Alternately, slice 1½ pounds of fish filet thinly. Place in the marinade. When the congee is cooked, add fish slices and marinade and allow congee to come to a boil. The fish will cook instantly. Turn off heat, pour congee into a heated tureen, garnish and serve. For this alternate, filleted sole or flounder may be used.

Preserved Egg and Pork Congee

(Pei Dan Ham Sau Yook Jook)

1 recipe Congee (without salt) (page 22)

1½ cups Salted Pork (page 18), cut into strips 2 inches long, ½ inch wide and ¼ inch thick

3 preserved eggs (see Note, below), shelled, cut coarsely into ½-inch pieces

4 tablespoons Scallion Oil (page 16)

½ cup scallions, trimmed, finely sliced

Salt, to taste

As the congee is cooking, prepare the salted pork and the preserved eggs.

About 20 minutes before the congee is finished cooking, add scallion oil. Stir and mix well. Add pork and preserved eggs, mix thoroughly and allow to simmer for 20 minutes until well blended. Add scallions, stir in well. Turn off heat, taste and add salt if necessary. Transfer to a heated tureen and serve immediately.

MAKES 6 SERVINGS

N O T E Preserved eggs are often called thousand-year-old eggs. Once they had been coated with clay and husks of grain, and came packed in huge ceramic clay barrels, from which they were sold. Today they are clean, their shells are gray, they are individually wrapped in plastic and packed six to a box.

These recipes, traditional bedrock basics, were taught first by my grandmother to demonstrate that cooking must be done properly and that shortcuts were forbidden. Even though I occasionally modify recipes for the modern kitchen, the philosophy behind them is constant. In these early days of learning, my Ah Paw would say repeatedly, *"Soi guah op bui. Soi guah op bui,"* or "Water passes easily over a duck's back feathers," which indicated that if a person failed to listen to explicit instructions, her work would be poor. This pertained particularly to kitchen disciplines, she said, and I would be wise to listen closely.

That brick kitchen where I began to cook in China differs only in degrees of modernity from my kitchen today, and not at all in its basics. That wood-burning stove in front of which I stood on a stool and stir-fried with an iron spatula in a cast-iron wok held by one of my grandmother's servants, has been replaced by a stainless steel six-burner gas stove—similar to those used in commercial restaurants. Those thin cast-iron woks that often burned through have evolved into carbon steel woks that last for decades. Instead of bamboo sticks stretched across a wok supporting foods to be steamed over boiling water, there are now bamboo, aluminum and steel steamers. But all of the processes are the same.

The woks used in Ah Paw's kitchen were of thin cast iron that with constant use, often burned through and had to be patched and repaired by traveling *foh wok*— itinerant metal workers, who went from town to town. Today there are carbon steel woks which, after seasoning with cooking oil, require little interior washing and cook beautifully with the merest amounts of oil, and last indefinitely. There are woks of stainless steel and aluminum as well, good for steaming, less so for stir-frying. Woks are one- and two-handled, flat-bottomed and round. In my collection of more than two dozen woks, which range in size from twelve to twenty-four inches in diameter, I even have one old cast-iron wok, simply to remind myself of my grandmother's kitchen.

Carbon steel ladles and spatulas have remained unchanged in fifty years, but those of iron have been replaced with stainless steel, and they're lighter and more efficient. I still use wire mesh strainers from as small as four inches across to as large as fourteen inches, but I now also have wide, round strainers of steel punched through with holes, almost like colanders with handles. The heavy iron and steel alloy cleavers used in Ah Paw's kitchen have been replaced by a wide variety of cleavers, carbon steel and stainless, with wood handles; others are made of one-piece honed steel, light for slicing and dicing, heavy for chopping through bone. The best one, the one used in the kitchens of the best Chinese chefs, is an American-made well-balanced cleaver by Dexter.

As you will note even the changes in Chinese cooking implements has been a slow evolution, more modernization than change. Yet basically, all has remained the same throughout history. I still mince meats for dumpling fillings with my cleaver as I learned to in Ah Paw's kitchen. I remember her dictum about washing a cutting board thoroughly so that subsequent foods cut on it would remain pure in their inherent flavors and blend seamlessly. Foods would not be cohesive she told me, if perfect cleanliness was not adhered to. I remember when she instructed me on how to concoct the stuffing for bitter melon, one of our family's favorite foods. I knew the seasonings involved: salt, pepper, sugar, soy sauce, oyster sauce, sliced scallions, ginger juice, white rice wine, a touch of cornstarch. These were to be combined with perfectly minced fresh shrimp.

I minced, mixed, stirred the mass in one direction only, as my grandmother had instructed. I stuffed the melon slices, cooked them. At dinner that night, after everyone had eaten and said they enjoyed the bitter melon, Ah Paw asked for quiet and announced that Ah Fei, at the age of eight, had made the dish *jiu tak ho* perfectly, and that the family should congratulate her. I was so proud. That is how it was in my grandmother's kitchen, how it has been for my children when they have cooked properly and well, and not *bun san suk,* defined by my grandmother as "half cooked, half not cooked." It is how it will be for my granddaughter, and yours as well.

TO THE MARKET

去
市
場

ONE OF MY MANY DISCOVERIES AS a young girl was the market in Ah Paw's town of Sah Gau. Because it was a large town, much larger than my small village of Siu Lo Chin, it was the market town for many surrounding villages as well; it contained many shops, and was filled with smells, sweet and savory. My grandmother insisted that shopping for her household meals was a twice-daily affair. I would sit with her as we finished breakfast, then would consult with Dai Kum Moh, my number-one aunt, who lived in one of Ah Paw's four houses but ate with us. Then she called in Ah Guk, my aunt's more experienced servant and shopper. My aunt supervised all of Ah Paw's food shopping because she knew virtually all the shopkeepers quite well, and preferred to shop with Ah Guk, whom she respected. Often I would go with them.

The Sah Gau market was a collection of streets and alleys filled with dozens of shops, and each had to be visited because virtually every food that we needed to buy was sold loose, by weight. There were no bottles of oil, or vinegar, or wines, or any other of our liquid staples such as soy sauce, oyster sauce, sesame oil and hoisin sauce. There were no packages of water chestnuts or sugar, salt, flours, dried shrimp and cuttlefish or salted fish. Everything, liquid or solid, was sold by the tael and catty. Ah Guk, whose name translated to Chrysanthemum, would carry a collection of bottles and jars, which needed to be filled on each trip.

One tael equaled 1.3 ounces, with twelve taels equivalent to a pound; one catty of sixteen taels equaled twenty-two ounces. Shops had measuring cups for the dried foods, and ladles of varying sizes for the liquids. One shop I recall had a huge clay pot containing a mound of fresh salt, harvested from the sea, still a bit moist. Next to it were barrels of loose brown sugar, slices of sugarcane sugar, and white sugar. Rice barrels contained extra-long-grain rice, short-grain, special rice from Thailand and glutinous rice. Barrels of soy sauce, oyster sauce, bean sauce, peanut oil and sesame paste stood alongside.

Another shop would have mounds of dried foods, both grown and baby shrimp, cloud ear fungus, tiger lily buds, mushrooms, dried scallops and mussels and bean thread noodles fashioned from mung beans. Various flours milled from water chestnuts and tapioca, from wheat and rice, and from the mung beans that provided much of our starch were displayed as well as a bewildering array of spices and herbs, all loose and unpacked.

Butchers sold mostly pork, in pieces, with every part of every pig seemingly finding a taker. There was some beef for the adventurous but most people ate pork exclusively. They sold *lop cheung*, the special pork and pork liver sausages, roasted duck and, at certain times of the year, cured slab bacon as well. Poultry shops sold freshly killed chickens, ducks and geese, fresh chicken and duck eggs as well as those preserved so-called thousand-year-old eggs.

Bean curd, always fresh, was made by the hour in small streetside factories and we would buy cakes, or smooth custards, or pieces of somewhat firm masses either in milky white or yellow. There was no difference—the yellow was simply dyed, for those people who might wish to serve yellow instead of white. Other shops lined up big crocks of white rice wines and the sherrylike Shao-Hsing, with them white and red distilled wine vinegars, and that special, thick balsamiclike Chinkiang vinegar. It was a true culinary cornucopia and I loved its smells as well as the small lengths of sweet sugarcane shopkeepers would give me to chew on.

With each visit the empty jars, bottles and crocks we brought to the market empty were returned to Ah Paw's house, filled, along with paper-wrapped parcels of dry goods. My number-one aunt loved the market bartering ritual. She would joke with the shopkeepers, pretend they were asking too high a price, that perhaps a soy sauce suggested was not from the smooth and balanced top of the fermented crock, but closer to the bean sauce that came from the soy crock bottom. She would heft a piece of pork, tell a storekeeper that his measurement of salt or white pepper seemed to be a bit less than the specified number of taels. But it was all in good humor, accepted by buyer and seller as part of market life, and when we returned to Ah Paw's house my grandmother and my aunt would laugh about that day's adventure.

These days, to be sure, all of those foods, spices and flavorings, all those oils and sauces and wines are available in bottles, jars and parcels, and shopping for foods remains a pleasure, but often I yearn for those stores and their smells.

Then it was to Ah Paw's kitchen for the preparation of that day's lunch and dinner, and of course my continued lessons. This day Ah Guk, at Ah Paw's instructions, was to teach me how to blanch foods and steam them, and I was to continue my practice in stir-frying.

BLANCHING AND STEAMING

Blanching is a process wherein foods are plunged into boiling water or oil, usually for mere seconds. With vegetables, blanching in boiling water, with a bit of salt added, serves to remove the water in the vegetables, heightens their color, and tenderizes them without softening their texture. The process, according to my grandmother, was called *chut soi*, which translates as "let the water out." The addition of a bit of baking soda to the water will brighten the color even more.

Blanching in oil, called *jau yau*, is usually reserved for meats, poultry and seafood, where the process serves to seal in the food's juices. Often vegetables that are deemed tough, such as bamboo shoots, jicama, water chestnuts and root vegetables are blanched in oil to keep their moisture in. Occasionally meats, poultry and shellfish are water-blanched as well, to remove their moisture. The methods of blanching are detailed in this book.

Steaming foods in my grandmother's kitchen was an exercise in saving time, energy and extra effort. Often we steamed foods by setting them atop rice in woks so that they would cook along with the rice. These days steaming is a different practice, though the principle is the same. Foods are placed in steamproof dishes, set on racks over boiling water, covered and steamed for specific times. Steaming can be done in traditional bamboo steamers set into woks over boiling water or in steel and aluminum pots with steaming inserts. The process, called *jing*, preserves the juices of the food in the steaming dishes, gives foods a natural, glistening appearance, and is the perfect process for reheating. When steaming, boiling water should be kept on hand to replenish any that evaporates.

Every day, including shopping days, complete meals would be cooked both for lunch and for dinner in Ah Paw's house. When I was permitted to stir-fry, the essential cooking process of the Chinese kitchen, my grandmother would caution me, virtually every time, with *sin lok ngan hau lok yuen,* which iterated that in the stir-fry, hard foods always went into the wok first, the soft foods later. By the time I was eight years old I was stir-frying with confidence, and always remembering hard first, soft second.

There were always seven or eight people at my grandmother's table, my number-one aunt, to be sure, the servants, my grandmother and me, and any of the relatives who occupied her other houses who happened to be in Sah Gau. Each meal, lunch or dinner, was equally as important as another.

Steamed Black Mushrooms

(Jing Dong Gu)

This versatile mushroom preparation is wonderful at any time, eaten as they are just out of the steamer, or as part of a large banquet, or as an ingredient in other dishes. They may be eaten hot or cold.

24 Chinese dried black mushrooms, about 1½ inches in diameter

¾ teaspoon salt

2 teaspoons sugar

1½ tablespoons dark soy sauce

1½ tablespoons oyster sauce

2 tablespoons Shao-Hsing wine, or sherry

2 teaspoons sesame oil

3 tablespoons Scallion Oil (page 16)

½ cup Vegetable Stock (page 14)

3 scallions, trimmed, cut into 2-inch pieces

1 slice fresh ginger, 1 inch thick, lightly smashed

Soak mushrooms in hot water for 30 to 45 minutes, until softened. Wash thoroughly and squeeze out excess water. Remove stems and place mushrooms in a steamproof dish. Add all other ingredients to the mushrooms. Place steamproof dish in a steamer, cover and steam for 30 minutes. (See steaming directions, page 30.)

Turn off heat and remove dish from steamer. Discard the scallions and ginger and gently toss mushrooms in remaining liquid. Serve hot immediately, or allow to cool before serving. The mushrooms will keep, refrigerated and covered with plastic wrap, for 4 to 5 days.

SERVES 4 TO 6

Steamed Black Mushrooms Braised with Bean Curd and Tianjin Bok Choy

(Dong Gu Dau Fu Kau Jun Choy)

冬菇豆腐扣津菜

This preparation relies upon firm bean curd, to ensure that it does not come apart while cooking. This is one of those dishes that proceeded from my grandmother's kitchen, through my mother's kitchen, to mine.

SAUCE

2 tablespoons oyster sauce

2 teaspoons light soy sauce

1 teaspoon sesame oil

1½ tablespoons Shao-Hsing wine, or sherry

1½ teaspoons sugar

¼ teaspoon salt

2 tablespoons cornstarch

Pinch white pepper

3 tablespoons Steamed Black Mushroom liquid (page 32)

3 tablespoons peanut oil

1 tablespoon minced ginger

¼ teaspoon salt

1 head fresh Tianjin bok choy (Napa cabbage) washed, drained, dried, and cut into:

    4 cups stalks, cut across into ½-inch strips

    5 cups leaves, cut across into ½-inch strips

6 Steamed Black Mushrooms, cut into thin strips

½ cup Vegetable Stock (page 14)

2 cakes firm fresh bean curd, cut into ½-inch strips

½ cup red bell peppers, cut into 2-inch by ⅛-inch strips

In a small bowl, combine all ingredients for sauce; set aside.

Heat wok over high heat for 30 seconds. Add peanut oil and coat wok with spatula. When a wisp of white smoke appears, add ginger and salt, stir for 30 seconds. Add bok choy stalks, stir and cook for 2 minutes. Add leaves, stir and cook for 2 minutes more. Add mushrooms and stir mixture together.

Add stock, stir and braise for 4 to 5 minutes, until stalks soften. As mixture cooks, toss 2 to 3 times. Add bean curd, stir and allow to come to a boil. Stir sauce, pour into mixture and stir well until sauce thickens and bubbles, about 2 minutes. Add peppers, stir and mix for 1 minute. Turn off heat and serve immediately with cooked rice.

SERVES 4 TO 6

Steamed Black Mushrooms and Chicken Ding

(Don Gu Gai Ding)

One afternoon when I was about eight years old, Ah Paw said to me, "Ah Fei, it is time for you to make a ding." A ding, she explained was a special way of preparing foods by cutting them into small cubes, before cooking; a method, she said, that was favored by Confucius.

SAUCE

2½ tablespoons oyster sauce

1 tablespoon dark soy sauce

2 teaspoons sesame oil

2 teaspoons sugar

¼ teaspoon salt

2 tablespoons Shao-Hsing wine, or sherry

Pinch white pepper

⅔ cup Chicken Stock (page 13)

2 tablespoons Chicken Stock

1½ tablespoons cornstarch

3 tablespoons peanut oil

½ teaspoon salt

2 teaspoons minced ginger

2 teaspoons minced garlic

½ cup onions, cut into ¼-inch dice

3 scallions, trimmed, cut into ¼-inch pieces diagonally, separate white and green portions

1 cup Steamed Black Mushrooms (page 32), cut into ⅓-inch cubes

6 cakes (1¼ pounds) firm bean curd, or 1 package of 4 cakes, 18 ounces, drained, cut into ½-inch cubes

2 tablespoons coriander, finely sliced

Prepare sauce mixture and reserve. Combine 2 tablespoons stock with cornstarch; set aside.

Heat wok over high heat for 45 seconds. Add peanut oil, coat wok with spatula. When a wisp of white smoke appears, add salt, ginger and garlic, mix. When garlic releases its fragrance, add onions. Cook for 1 minute. Add white portions of scallions and toss mixture together. Add mushrooms and cook for 1 minute. Add bean curd, mix well.

Add the reserved sauce mixture to the wok, stir well and cook for 5 to 7 minutes until bean curd absorbs the liquid. Make a well in the mix, stir cornstarch mixture, pour in and stir until mixture thickens, 1½ to 2 minutes. Add green portions of scallions and coriander and mix thoroughly. Turn off heat, transfer to a heated dish and serve immediately with cooked rice

SERVES 4 TO 6

Stir-Fried Pork with Steamed Black Mushrooms and Onions

(Dong Gu Yeung Chung Chau Yuk See)

冬
菇
洋
蔥
炒
肉
絲

There were differences in vegetables, my grandmother taught me. For example, in this traditional dish of pork, steamed mushrooms and onions, she pointed out the differences in onions. Those that were white and new contained much water; those that were yellow were older. Use the older ones, she taught, because they would give the stir-fry a crisp texture. She was right, as always.

MARINADE

1½ tablespoons oyster sauce

1½ teaspoons sesame oil

2 teaspoons light soy sauce

¾ teaspoon ginger juice mixed with 2 teaspoons Chinese white rice wine, or gin

2 teaspoons cornstarch

Pinch white pepper

1 teaspoon sugar

⅛ teaspoon salt

¾ pound fresh lean pork loin, cut into 2-inch by ¼-inch julienne

SAUCE

1 tablespoon oyster sauce

1½ teaspoons light soy sauce

1 teaspoon sesame oil

1 teaspoon sugar

Pinch white pepper

2 teaspoons cornstarch

2 teaspoons Chinese white rice wine, or gin

¼ cup Chicken Stock (page 13)

3½ tablespoons peanut oil

1 tablespoon minced ginger

⅛ teaspoon salt

1½ cups onions, julienned

¾ cup Steamed Black Mushrooms (page 32), julienned

⅔ cup bamboo shoots, julienned

½ cup scallions green portions only, julienned

2 teaspoons minced garlic

1 tablespoon Chinese white rice wine, or gin

Combine all marinade ingredients and add to it the pork; reserve. Mix all ingredients for sauce in a bowl and set aside.

Heat wok over high heat for 40 seconds, add 1½ tablespoons peanut oil, coat wok with spatula. When a wisp of white smoke appears, add ginger and salt and stir. Add onions, stir and cook for 1 minute. Add mushrooms, stir and cook for another minute. Add bamboo shoots, and mix well. Add scallions, stir and cook for 1 minute. Remove mixture from heat, transfer to a dish and reserve.

Wipe off wok and spatula. Heat wok over high heat for 30 seconds, add remaining 2 tablespoons peanut oil and coat wok. When a wisp of white smoke appears, add garlic, stir. When garlic releases its fragrance, add pork and marinade. Spread in a thin layer, tip wok side to side to cook evenly. When pork begins to turn white, turn over, mix well. Drizzle the wine into the wok along its edges, stir to mix, cook until pork turns white. Add reserved vegetables, stir and mix thoroughly. Make a well in the center of the mixture, stir sauce, pour in and mix well to combine. When sauce thickens and the pork is well coated, about 1 to 1½ minutes, turn off heat. Taste to ensure that the cornstarch is cooked through and there is no floury taste. If necessary, stir-fry another 30 to 45 seconds. Turn off heat, transfer to a heated dish and serve immediately with cooked rice.

SERVES 4 TO 6

Five-Spice Kau Yuk

(Ng Heung Kau Yuk)

This was a favorite of Ah Paw's. Its name defies English translation. The words *kau yuk* translate loosely as long-cooked, or stewed, fresh bacon or pork belly. Fresh, or uncured, it was available year-round in the butcher shops. This dish of fresh bacon is flavored with five different spices and cooked several hours until the meat has softened and absorbed its cooking liquid, and much of its fat has run off. It is a true heirloom dish cooked in the way it has been for generations without alterations. Only occasionally do its flavorings change. This kau yuk of my grandmother's will be passed, unchanged, on to my granddaughter.

In our family this kau yuk was traditionally served with Chinese broccoli and cooked rice.

6½ cups cold water

4½ ounces sugarcane sugar or dark brown sugar

1 piece ginger, 1½ inches long, lightly smashed

4 scallions, trimmed, cut in half

3 cinnamon sticks 3 inches long

4 pieces 8-star anise

10 cloves

¼ teaspoon anise seeds

¼ teaspoon Sichuan peppercorns

2 to 2½ pounds fresh bacon, left in 1 piece (Usually cut by Chinese butchers into a piece about 11 inches long, 2½ inches wide, about 2½ inches thick. There will be two ribs attached, which should be left on. Tie the meat around four times along its length, which will prevent the meat from falling apart during the cooking.)

⅔ cup double dark soy sauce

⅔ cup Shao-Hsing wine, or sherry

Place water, sugar, ginger, scallions and five spices into a large pot. Stir to blend, add bacon. Cover and bring to a boil over high heat. As it boils, add soy sauce and stir.

Return to a boil, add Shao-Hsing wine and mix. Return again to a boil. Lower heat, cover pot, leaving a slight opening at the lid and simmer for 4 hours.

As it simmers, turn meat over 8 times, so that each of the 4 sides cooks through. Turn off heat. Close lid and allow meat to come to room temperature. Place entire contents of pot into a large bowl and refrigerate overnight. This allows the meat to further absorb the spices.

TO SERVE: Remove meat from refrigerator to a chopping board. Cut off string, remove ribs and discard. Cut meat across into ⅓-inch slices and allow to come to room temperature. Place slices in a steamproof dish, ladle sauce over slices and steam for 10 to 12 minutes until very hot. (See steaming directions, page 30.) Serve immediately.

MAKES 4 SERVINGS

Chinese Broccoli

(Gai Lan)

Chinese broccoli differs greatly from the broccoli most people are familiar with. Its stalks are long and green, and its dark green leaves do not resemble broccoli florets, rather they are true leaves. When bought in Asian markets the bunches usually display both small white flowers and green buds. The fewer flowers, the more tender the broccoli. After buying, the broccoli should be prepared immediately since it tends to flower and become tougher quite quickly.

To prepare, remove old top tough leaves, cut off flowers and buds. Peel green outer layers from stalks, to reveal tender insides. Chinese broccoli is widely available these days.

> 8 cups water
>
> 1 slice ginger, ½ inch thick, lightly smashed
>
> 1 tablespoon salt
>
> ¾ teaspoon baking soda (optional)
>
> 1 bunch Chinese broccoli, trimmed, peeled, yield 1 pound

Place water, ginger and salt in a large pot and bring to a boil over high heat. Add baking soda before water comes to a boil. Water-blanch broccoli for 1 minute. It will turn bright green in seconds, but continue to blanch to make it tender. Remove from water, immerse in ice water to halt cooking. Drain well.

Cut individual stalks in half and arrange in a steamproof dish. Place kau yuk slices, skin side up, atop the broccoli. Spoon sauce over kau yuk and broccoli. Steam for 10 minutes until both are very hot. (See steaming directions, page 30.) Serve with cooked rice.

SERVES 4

Bok Choy with Chinese Bacon

(Bok Choy Chau Lop Yuk)

白菜炒腊肉

Cured Chinese bacon, also sold in butcher shops, was available only in the winter months. It was a particular preparation, cured with a so-called *Ji Yau*, or "pearl sauce," made from a very thick, dark and sweet soy sauce, wine and salt, then dried in the sun. These days it is oven-dried. But in Ah Paw's day, Chinese bacon was a seasonal anticipated treat.

SAUCE

1 tablespoon soy sauce

1 teaspoon dark soy sauce

⅓ cup Chicken Stock (page 13)

1 tablespoon cornstarch

⅔ cup cured Chinese bacon, thinly sliced, with fatty portions separated from portions striped with meat

1 slice ginger, ½ inch thick, lightly smashed

¼ teaspoon salt

1¼ pounds bok choy, washed, dried, leaves and stalks separated, cut into 1-inch pieces

Combine all ingredients for sauce in a small bowl; set aside.

Heat wok over high heat for 40 seconds. Place fatty portions of bacon in wok, cook for 1 minute. Add remainder of bacon, cook 1 to 2 minutes until bacon browns. Remove bacon from wok, reserve. Leave bacon fat in wok.

Raise heat, add ginger and salt, stir. When ginger turns light brown, add white bok choy stalks and stir-fry for 2 minutes. Add bok choy leaves and stir-fry for 1 minute more. If too dry, sprinkle a little cold water in wok to create steam. The leaves should turn bright green. Make a well in the mixture, stir sauce, pour in and mix thoroughly until sauce thickens and turns dark brown. Add reserved bacon, mix well until hot. Remove to a heated dish, serve immediately with cooked rice.

SERVES 4

Barbecued Pork

(Char Siu)

This cooked pork was bought in the market most often, but occasionally, as a treat for Ah Paw's table, it would be roasted on the small, charcoal-fired ceramic stove that sat on a bench in the open area off Ah Paw's kitchen. We loved the meat for its versatility. It could be eaten as a sliced snack, as an appetizer, a first course, stir-fried with other foods or as a perfect addition to fried rice. It was eaten hot or at room temperature. Here is how I make it, in my oven.

4½ pounds pork loin

MARINADE

3 tablespoons dark soy sauce

3 tablespoons light soy sauce

½ cup honey

1 teaspoon salt

4 tablespoon oyster sauce

3 tablespoons Shao-Hsing wine, or sherry

4 tablespoons hoisin sauce

⅛ teaspoon white pepper

2 cakes wet preserved bean curd (page 245), mashed

1½ teaspoons five-spice powder

Quarter the pork loin lengthwise. Using a small knife, pierce each length repeatedly at 2-inch intervals, to tenderize. Line a roasting pan with foil, arrange lengths of pork in a single layer. Combine marinade ingredients. Pour over pork and allow to marinate at least 4 hours, or overnight.

Preheat oven to Broil. Place pork loin in a roasting pan and roast 30 to 50 minutes. During cooking time, meat should be basted 5 or 6 times and turned 4 times. To test, remove one strip after 30 minutes, slice it to see if it is cooked through. If sauce dries out, add some boiling water to pan. When cooked, allow pork to rest 3 to 4 minutes, then serve. Or allow to cool, then refrigerate until further use. It will keep, refrigerated 4 to 5 days, and can be frozen for as long as 3 months. Allow to defrost or come to room temperature before use.

Barbecued Pork Ribs

(Siu Pai Guat)

I prepare barbecued pork spareribs similarly to Barbecued Pork (43). These were never made in Ah Paw's house, but they have been for years in mine, to the delight of my children, and now to that of my granddaughter. The marinade differs, but cooking them is similar to cooking *Char Siu*.

1 3- to 3½-pound rack pork spareribs

MARINADE

3 tablespoons hoisin sauce

3 tablespoons oyster sauce

2½ tablespoons light soy sauce

2½ tablespoons dark soy sauce

4 tablespoons honey

2 tablespoons Shao-Hsing wine, or sherry

¾ teaspoon salt

Pinch white pepper

Remove flap and layer of fat from the rack of ribs, then with a sharp knife, score the rack all over. Line roasting pan with heavy-duty foil, arrange rack of ribs inside. Mix marinade ingredients together. Using your hands rub marinade thoroughly into spareribs. Allow to marinate at least 4 hours, or covered, refrigerated overnight. Bring to room temperature before roasting.

Preheat oven to broil, 500 to 550 degrees F. Broil ribs for approximately 40 minutes, adding boiling water to pan if sauce dries out. During cooking, baste ribs several times, and turn over rack several times until done. To test, slice into thick, meaty portion of rack. Meat is cooked through when no redness shows. Turn off heat, cut ribs between bones and meat, and serve.

MAKES 12 RIBS

Pork Ribs Siu Mai

(Pai Guat Siu Mai)

These spareribs were eaten often in Ah Paw's house simply because they were easily steamed after being butchered. The butcher would trim the flap, cut each rib and its meat individually, then chop each rib into 1-inch sections, giving us a pile of small pieces of ribs.

MARINADE

1 teaspoon sesame oil

2 teaspoons salt

2 tablespoons sugar

1 tablespoon Chinese white rice wine, or gin

2 tablespoons oyster sauce

1 tablespoon minced garlic

3 tablespoons fermented black beans, washed

¾ teaspoon baking soda

4 tablespoons tapioca flour

Pinch white pepper

½ teaspoon hot pepper flakes

1 rack pork ribs, to yield after butchering: 3 cups of ribs, or 2½ pounds

2 tablespoons fresh bell peppers, diced

Mix marinade well in a large bowl. Place sparerib pieces in a steamproof dish. Pour in marinade, mix to coat well. Allow to marinate for 8 hours or overnight, in the refrigerator. Before steaming, allow to come to room temperature.

Place steamproof dish in a steamer, cover and steam for 30 minutes, or until done. (See steaming directions, page 30.) Remove dish from steamer, sprinkle with red peppers and serve immediately.

SERVES 4 TO 6

Chicken Braised with Black Beans

(Dau See Mun Gai)

This dish is special because the chicken is cooked three times. It is a recipe that takes a bit of work, but as my grandmother said, it is worth the effort, both in the kitchen and at the table.

6 garlic cloves, lightly smashed, peeled and mashed

5 tablespoons fermented black beans, washed several times to remove salt, drained well

SAUCE

3 tablespoons oyster sauce

2 teaspoons sugar

½ teaspoon salt

2 tablespoons dark soy sauce

1 3½-pound chicken washed well with salt, fat and membranes removed, drained and dried thoroughly

3½ to 4 tablespoons water chestnut powder

6 cups plus 3 tablespoons peanut oil

3 tablespoons Chinese white rice wine, or gin

1 cup Chicken Stock (page 13)

Sprigs of coriander, for garnish

Make a paste of the mashed garlic and black beans, reserve. Mix sauce, reserve.

Cut chicken into bite-size pieces, coat with water chestnut powder. Heat wok over high heat for 1 minute. Add 6 cups peanut oil and heat to 375 degrees F, until oil smokes. Deep-fry the chicken pieces by lowering them into the oil with a Chinese strainer. Fry 1 minute, or until redness is gone from the skin. Remove chicken, drain, reserve. Drain oil from wok, wipe dry with paper towels.

Place remaining 3 tablespoons peanut oil in wok over high heat and when a wisp of white smoke appears, add the garlic–black bean paste. Break up with spatula. When garlic turns light brown, add chicken pieces and mix well. Drizzle white wine into wok from edges, stir and mix well. Stir sauce, pour into wok, mix until chicken is well-coated. Turn off heat.

Transfer chicken to a pot. Pour ¾ cup chicken stock into wok to help collect juices and sauce, then pour into pot over chicken. Cover pot and cook over low heat until chicken is tender, 30 to 40 minutes, stirring every 10 minutes. If sauce becomes too thick, add a bit more stock, 1 to 2 tablespoons at a time.

Turn off heat, remove chicken and sauce from pot and transfer to a heated dish. Garnish with coriander and serve with cooked rice.

SERVES 4 TO 6

Chicken with Hot Bean Sauce

(Dau Bang Jeung Chau Gai See)

According to Ah Paw, the moderate spiciness of this dish reduced the body's dampness, particularly in the March rainy season. Often she would reject chiles as being too hot, but this sauce gave heat without discomfort to the tongue, she said, and therefore was what she termed *lot lot dei*, or pleasing hot.

MARINADE

2 tablespoons egg whites, lightly beaten

½ teaspoon salt

2 tablespoons tapioca starch

1 pound chicken cutlets, cut into 2½-by-⅓-inch strips

SAUCE

2½ tablespoons hot bean sauce

2½ tablespoons oyster sauce

1 tablespoon light soy sauce

1 tablespoon sugar

1 tablespoon Shao-Hsing wine, or sherry

1 tablespoon Chinkiang vinegar

1 teaspoon sesame oil

Pinch white pepper

1 tablespoon tapioca starch

⅓ cup Chicken Stock (page 13)

5 cups peanut oil, for blanching

2 teaspoons minced ginger

2 teaspoons minced garlic

¼ cup scallions, white portions only, cut diagonally into ¼-inch slices

½ pound red bell peppers, cut into 2-inch by ¼-inch strips

1 tablespoon Shao-Hsing wine, or sherry

Combine all marinade ingredients; place chicken strips in marinade, mix well to coat and allow to rest 15 minutes. Reserve.

While chicken marinates, combine all sauce ingredients in a bowl. Set aside.

Heat wok over high heat for 1 minute. Add 5 cups peanut oil and bring to a temperature of 300 degrees F. Add chicken and marinade. Turn off heat immediately, loosen chicken strips to separate them. When chicken is loosened, turn heat on to medium. When chicken turns white (about 45 seconds), turn off heat, remove with strainer, and drain over a bowl.

Empty wok of oil, leaving about 2 tablespoons in well. Turn heat to high and heat for 20 seconds. Add ginger and garlic, stir. Add scallions and cook for 45 seconds. Add peppers, stir together, cook 2 minutes. Add chicken, mix together. Drizzle wine into wok from the edges. Make a well, stir sauce, pour into wok, and stir thoroughly. When sauce thickens and bubbles, turn off heat. Transfer to a heated dish and serve with cooked rice.

SERVES 4

Roast Duck

(Siu Op)

Whereas my grandmother raised chickens, ducks were raised by farmers, not only for their meat, but for their prized eggs, eaten fresh, salted or preserved. When Ah Paw decided that the family was to have duck, Ah Guk would be sent to the market to buy one already roasted. Freshly killed ducks were a special treat reserved generally for festivals, family feasts and special occasions. Cooked ducks roasted to a glistening brown were hung in store windows, as they are today in Chinatown shops, as enticing adornments. Usually they would be cut up to order, as desired, and brought home to be used in combinations with other foods. Or they may be bought whole, as Ah Paw preferred, and skinned, boned and cut up as she desired. After roasting, a five-pound duck would weigh a bit more than three pounds. The duck, after being skinned and boned would yield about 3 cups of meat, sufficient for two recipes, such as these.

The first dish is notable for its use of cashew nuts, which the Chinese call *eel guor*, descriptively "kidney fruit."

Roast Duck Ding

(Siu Op Ding)

SAUCE

2½ tablespoons oyster sauce

2 teaspoons light soy sauce

1½ teaspoons sesame oil

1½ teaspoons Chinkiang vinegar

1 tablespoon Chinese white rice wine, or gin

4½ teaspoons sugar

Pinch white pepper

3½ teaspoons cornstarch

¼ cup Chicken Stock (page 13)

2½ cups peanut oil, for deep-frying

¾ cup raw cashew nuts

1 tablespoon minced ginger

⅛ teaspoon salt

1 cup (¼ pound) long beans or stringbeans, cut into ½-inch pieces

½ cup celery, cut into ⅓-inch dice

⅓ cup bamboo shoots, cut into ⅓-inch dice

⅓ cup water chestnuts, cut into ⅓-inch dice

¾ cup red bell pepper, cut into ½-inch dice

2½ teaspoons minced garlic

1½ cups roast duck meat (Cut whole duck in half, lengthwise. Reserve half for subsequent dish. Remove skin, fat and bones, cut meat into ½-inch dice.)

1½ tablespoons Chinese white rice wine, or gin

In a small bowl, mix all ingredients for sauce; reserve.

Prepare cashews: Heat wok over high heat for 1 minute. Add peanut oil and heat to 340–350 degrees F. Add cashews, stir and fry for 1 to 1½ minutes until golden. Remove with strainer, drain, reserve. Empty oil from wok.

Heat wok over high heat and return 1½ tablespoons of oil to wok. Add ginger and salt, stir 30 seconds. Add beans, stir and cook for 1 minute. Add celery, stir and cook for 30 seconds. Add bamboo shoots, stir and cook for 1 minute. Add water chestnuts, stir and cook 30 seconds. Add peppers, stir and cook for 1 minute. Turn off heat and remove to a dish, reserve.

Wipe off wok and spatula. Heat wok over high heat, add 2 tablespoons of reserved oil and coat wok. When a wisp of white smoke appears, add garlic, stir for 30 seconds, until garlic releases its fragrance. Add duck meat and stir, 1 minute. Drizzle wine into wok along its edges and cook for 1 minute. Add reserved vegetables, stir and cook for 1½ minutes. Make a well in the mixture, stir sauce, pour in and mix thoroughly until sauce bubbles and all ingredients are well-coated. Turn off heat. Add reserved cashews, mix well. Transfer to a heated dish and serve with cooked rice.

SERVES 4 TO 6

NOTE The cashews may be fried in advance. Drain, cool and place in closed container. They will keep 2 days.

Roast Duck with Snow Peas

(Siu Op Chau Seut Dau)

燒
鴨
炒
雪
豆

SAUCE

2½ tablespoons oyster sauce

2 teaspoons light soy sauce

1½ teaspoons sesame oil

3½ teaspoons sugar

1 tablespoon Chinese white rice wine, or gin

Pinch white pepper

3 teaspoons cornstarch

¼ cup Chicken Stock (page 13)

3½ tablespoons peanut oil

⅛ teaspoon salt

1 tablespoon minced ginger

¾ cup scallions, white portions, cut into 2-inch sections, julienned

1¾ cups (6 ounces) snow peas, julienned

1 cup jicama, cut into 2-inch matchstick julienne

2½ teaspoons minced garlic

1 tablespoon Shao-Hsing wine, or sherry

1½ cups duck meat (from Roast Duck Ding, page 51, skinned, boned, meat shredded)

In a small bowl mix all ingredients for sauce; reserve.

Heat wok over high heat for 40 seconds. Add 1½ tablespoons peanut oil, coat wok with spatula. When a wisp of white smoke appears, add salt and ginger, stir for 30 seconds. Add scallions, stir and cook 10 seconds. Add snow peas, stir and cook for 1½ minutes, or until snow peas become bright green. Add jicama, stir and cook for 1½ minutes. Turn off heat, remove wok contents to a dish and reserve.

Wipe off wok and spatula. Add remaining 2 tablespoons of peanut oil. Heat wok over high heat 30 seconds. When a wisp of white smoke appears, add garlic and stir until garlic releases its fragrance, about 20–30 seconds. Add duck meat, stir and cook 1 minute. Drizzle wine into wok along its edges, stir and cook 1 minute. Add reserved vegetables, mix well and cook 1½ minutes. Make a well, stir sauce and pour in to wok. Stir, to coat all ingredients well and cook, about 1½ minutes. Turn off heat, transfer to a heated dish and serve with cooked rice.

SERVES 4

A Swallow Learns to Fly

After a year of school holidays, weekends and summer days spent in my grandmother's house, I found that I was able to cook with a measure of confidence, even though I was then just about nine years old. I could tell that what I was learning and doing pleased Ah Paw and one night, as I was sitting with her on her bed, she told me, "I am not surprised. *Sun tak yan ho lah sau ho sik jiu yeh,*" which translates literally as "The people of Sun Tak are highly skilled in their knowledge of food," but is widely understood to mean that if one is born in Sun Tak, she is born to cook. I was, of course, from Sun Tak, as was Ah Paw, and she added that I would not have any trouble at all finding a husband since I cooked so well already, and that as I grew older I would only become more expert.

"You know," Ah Paw said, "that your name, Yin-Fei, means Flying Swallow. It means you will fly. You are smart and you are pretty." I would work in her kitchen, learning, for as long as she wished, I thought, just to have her say things like that to me, and to sleep next to her at night.

THIS PHOTO WAS TAKEN JUST BEFORE I LEFT FOR HONG KONG, AT AGE 12.

THREE

IN THE GARDEN

AH PAW'S GARDEN WAS UNDER THE care of the Chan family. They were farmers: a man, his wife and their three sons, and after tending to their own small farm, they would come as a family to plant, weed and harvest Ah Paw's garden, for which they were paid. The Chans were also charged with seeing to Ah Paw's fish ponds in which carp were raised, as well as her large fields of sugarcane and mulberry bushes, which surrounded the ponds. To perhaps call that vast planted area a garden fails to do it justice. It was about the size of a modern-day football field, completely enclosed by a high brick wall, and could be entered only through the rear door of one of the houses Ah Paw owned, a short distance down the road on which her home rested.

Planted in its acres were individual patches of the vegetables we ate every day:

bok choy, choy sum, cabbages and kale, Chinese broccoli and eggplant, long beans, scallions, taro root, turnips, white radishes, cucumbers, silk squash, watercress, carrots, peppers, celery and peanuts. Wild tomatoes grew along the edges of its walls. Because of the generally warm climate in the south of China, there were often two crops of most of these vegetables each year. A grove of fruit trees occupied one corner of the garden: guavas, pomegranates, pomelos, chestnuts and peaches. I loved the garden, but mostly I loved the trees, which I climbed constantly.

Whenever I was able, I would run down the road, through the empty house that served as the gateway to the walled garden just to climb those trees. This, despite cautions from Ah Guk, my grandmother's servant who would shake a finger at me and say, *"M'ho hawk lam jai seung shu,"* or "Don't be like a boy and climb trees," or *"Siu sum ah, nei hai loi jai,"* "Be careful, you're a girl." These warnings, she would tell me, came straight from my grandmother, which I doubted, for when Ah Paw said much the same to me, it was with a little smile.

It was my grandmother who had me go into the fields with the Chans each October and learn to cut sugarcane, and I would share in the sweet red congee her servants cooked for the Chans and the other harvesters.

As was her practice with everything else, Ah Paw would tell the servants which vegetables were ripe to pick and to cook. No gingerroot, onions, garlic or potatoes were grown in her garden simply because they were deemed plentiful and quite inexpensive. And she refused to grow chives, leeks and shallots, because they were unholy.

When I first asked her why that was so, she said it was her belief, rooted in Buddhist folklore, and sat me down on her divan to tell me the story. Once there was in the land a corrupt official, a jealous man, who tried to turn the people away from one of their favorite generals. Unable to do so, the official and his wife falsely accused the general of high crimes. The general was tried by the official, found guilty and executed. However, the people could not be convinced and rose up and captured the official and his wife. They accused him of being the traitor, of killing a general who was patriotic, then paraded him and his wife through the crowds, stoned them, then fried them in a giant wok until they were nothing but ashes. When a wind arose, the ashes flew into a garden area and settled up the stalks of shallots, leeks and chives. The three vegetables were subsequently declared to be forbidden to Buddhist monks and nuns. Since that time, Ah Paw would say to me, *"Yun jung yau sam yeung jop,"* which translates as "In the garden three vegetables are unholy."

Today there is a continuing observance of this tale. To observe the death of the hated official and his wife, two lengths of dough were pressed together and deep-fried into a cruller, which was usually eaten with congee. To this day, these crullers are

A FAMILY PORTRAIT TAKEN IN THE GARDEN OF MY HOME IN SUN TAK IN THE EARLY
1980S. MY FATHER IS SEATED IN THE CENTER, SURROUNDED BY MY COUSIN,
HIS WIFE, AND THEIR CHILDREN.

called *yau jah guai*, or "deep-fried devil." To eat these with one's congee, Ah Paw
told me, was to remind oneself to be honest and straightforward, to be kind and never
harm another.

In the years I went to Ah Paw's house, listened to her, followed her dicta, it always
seemed that she would illustrate life's lessons and proper behavior with food as the
common denominator. I remember complaining to her once how tedious a task it was
to snap off the tiny hard ends of bean sprouts to get them ready for spring rolls. Her
reply? "If you wish to learn to make spring rolls well, you must learn the beginning of
the spring roll."

As a practicing Buddhist, my grandmother would eat only vegetables on the first
and fifteenth of each month, and for the first fifteen days of the month of the Lunar

MY GRANDMOTHER'S CHINESE KITCHEN

New Year. And she would eat lightly, usually a clear soup flavored with herbs and Chinese parsley, and some steamed vegetables. Otherwise she would spend these observant days sitting on her divan fingering her prayer beads and praying for her ancestors whose names were etched on flat sticks resting upon her family altar next to her couch. She told me this was her personal way of honoring Buddha.

Ah Paw was quick to point out that Buddha, through one of his high priests, showed wisdom when, to make up to humanity for the loss of chives, leeks and shallots, decreed that it was permissible for vegetarians to eat in their stead three specific shellfish: clams, mussels and oysters. The decree was, she said, *"hoi jung yau sam yeung,"* or "The ocean has three shelled creatures that are declared vegetarian." Indeed, these three were invariably served at meals during the New Year observance, and continue to be to this day.

When I would go into Ah Paw's garden to help pick vegetables for her tables, she would be strict. Take only leaves that were green, without any blackness at the edges, she instructed. Nor should there be any yellow in the leaves, for yellow was a sign that the vegetable was old, past its prime. Make certain leaves were not broken or snapped, she would say, and she would ask to see any roots pulled from the ground so she could look at the dirt for moisture.

She would tell me that scallions—*chun*—were particularly good vegetables because their name translates to wise. And they *were* wise, because their long, hollow stems indicated an open mind. As did the lotus, with holes in its root. Lettuce, *sahng choi*, was healthy, and as such was always served at birthday dinners. Broccoli was jade, and soy beans were inherently warming and, when cooked, became hot. I learned to cook vegetables without harming their inherent crispness, and I cook them identically to this day, whether stir-fried or steamed.

In Ah Paw's house we cooked and ate vegetables on their own, to be sure, but also in combination with pork in many forms, fresh or preserved, and with chicken, though never with beef, which is forbidden to Buddhists.

Stir-Fried Choi Sum

(Chau Choi Sum)

清炒菜心

Choi sum is a most delicious vegetable. Widely available in Asian markets, it has a bright green stem and leaves, and tiny yellow bud flowers. When cooked, it is very sweet. There is no Western equivalent for choi sum; simply ask for it by its Chinese name.

8 cups cold water

1 slice ginger, ¼ inch thick, lightly smashed

½ teaspoon baking soda, optional

2 bunches choi sum, washed, top tender portions broken off, about 4 to 5 inches, large leaves and flowers discarded

3 tablespoons peanut oil

½ teaspoon salt

2 teaspoons minced ginger

In a large pot place water, ginger slice and baking soda and bring to a boil over high heat. Add choi sum and water-blanch until it becomes bright green, about 1 minute. Turn off heat, remove pot from stove and pour through a strainer. Run choi sum under cold water for 1 minute, set aside. Drain thoroughly.

Heat wok over high heat, and peanut oil and salt and coat wok using spatula. Add minced ginger and stir. When ginger turns light brown, add drained choi sum. Stir-fry for 3 minutes, or until hot. Turn off heat, transfer to a heated dish and serve immediately.

SERVES 4 TO 6

Stir-Fried Watercress

(CHAU SEI YUNG CHOI)

 In America, watercress is not generally regarded as a vegetable of importance, but it is in China. Its pungent flavor is prized and it is stir-fried, made into soups, is often part of elaborate banquets and used as a decorative food, even as a bed or a garnish for other foods. My grandmother preferred to serve it unaccompanied, and so do I.

> 3 bunches fresh watercress, each bunch cut across in half, washed, drained
>
> 8 cups water
>
> 1 slice ginger, ¼ inch thick, lightly smashed
>
> ½ teaspoon baking soda, optional
>
> 2½ teaspoons salt
>
> 3 tablespoons peanut oil

In a pot place water, ginger, baking soda if using and 2 teaspoons salt, and bring to a boil over high heat. Immerse watercress and water-blanch for 30 seconds, until watercress turns bright green. Turn off heat, run cold water into pot, pour off and allow to drain for 10 to 15 minutes, tossing occasionally.

Heat a wok over high heat for 30 seconds. Add peanut oil and ½ teaspoon salt, coat wok with spatula. When a wisp of white smoke appears, add watercress. Use a chopstick to loosen the watercress if necessary. Stir-fry for 2 to 3 minutes, until hot. Turn off heat, transfer to a heated dish and serve immediately.

SERVES 4 TO 6

Stir-Fried Corn

(Chau Gum Jue)

In China, corn is known as *gum jue*, or "golden pearls." This vegetable gift from the West was grown in a large patch of my grandmother's walled garden, and was a treat eagerly awaited in summer. We always ate it fresh, often steamed atop rice, or cooked as a snack. As part of a larger meal, the kernels were usually stripped from the ear and stir-fried.

3½ teaspoons peanut oil

1½ teaspoons minced garlic

½ teaspoon salt

1½ tablespoons cold water

2½ cups fresh corn, stripped from the ear

¼ cup scallions, green portions only, finely sliced

Heat a wok over high heat for 30 seconds, add peanut oil and coat wok using a spatula. When a wisp of white smoke appears, add garlic and salt and stir, about 10 seconds. When garlic turns light brown, add corn, stir, cook for 1 minute. Add cold water, stir in. Cover wok and bring to a boil, about 2 to 3 minutes. Remove cover, stir corn. Lower heat, cover wok again and cook for 3 minutes more, or until corn is tender. Turn off heat, transfer to a heated dish, sprinkle with sliced scallions and serve immediately.

SERVES 4 TO 6

Ginger Pickle

(Wor Mei Dzi Geung)

和
味
子
薑

My grandmother's garden produced a variety of foods used as pickles and in salads. She did not care for cold foods of any kind, preferring her soups and other hot foods, but her family fancied pickles and salads, so they were made. From the garden came cucumber, jicama and turnips. From the market came gingerroot and mustard greens for pickling. This was another of the practices I learned in her kitchen, which I still use today. I pickle and make salads of turnips, Tianjin bok choy, cabbage and cauliflower, usually blanching them then curing them with a mix of water and vinegar, sugar and salt.

One of the most versatile pickles is made from fresh gingerroot. It was eaten as a snack, is an ingredient in many dishes, and as a garnish. In Ah Paw's house it was also eaten as the first course of a meal, in which we often paired it with those cured thousand-year-old eggs. The pickle is best made from young, pink fresh ginger when the sweetness of the sugar complements the subtle heat of the ginger.

MARINADE

1¼ teaspoons salt

¾ cup Chinese white rice vinegar, or distilled white vinegar

1 cup sugar

8 cups water

1 teaspoon baking soda (optional)

1½ pounds fresh young ginger, peeled (wash thoroughly and most of the thin outer brown barklike coating will come off) and cut into ⅛-inch slices

Mix all marinade ingredients in a bowl; reserve.

In a large pot bring water and baking soda to a boil over high heat. Add ginger slices and boil for 30 seconds. Remove from heat, add cold water to pot to stop cooking process, drain. Add cold water a second time, drain. Repeat a third time and allow ginger to sit in cold water for 10 minutes. Drain well, then place ginger slices in a bowl with the marinade, tossing well to coat.

Cover ginger and marinade, refrigerated, for at least 24 hours before serving. Serve cold. Ginger Pickle, placed in a tightly closed jar will keep, refrigerated, for at least 3 months.

MAKES ABOUT 1 ¼ POUNDS

Sour Turnip Salad

(Soon Lor Bok Salud)

酸
羅
蔔
沙
律

This very special pickle salad was reserved usually for memorable occasions such as weddings and the birthdays of grandparents, and was served always before meals because it was believed to stimulate the appetite.

1 2-pound Chinese turnip (white turnip), both ends cut off, discarded, peeled, washed, dried and cut in half lengthwise

1½ teaspoons salt

4 tablespoons sugar

4 tablespoons Chinese white rice vinegar, or distilled white vinegar

¼ teaspoon white pepper

Place each turnip half, cut side down, and cut along the length of each at ⅛-inch intervals. Do not cut all the way through, cut to ⅛-inch from the bottom (this will permit breaking off into half-moon slices), and cut each sliced half into 2-inch segments.

Place turnips in a bowl with salt, toss and allow to stand for 1 hour to let excess water drain. Discard water, add sugar, white vinegar and white pepper to bowl. Mix thoroughly and place bowl in refrigerator, covered with plastic wrap for at least 4 hours. Serve immediately. This salad will keep, refrigerated, for up to 2 days.

MAKES ABOUT 1¾ POUNDS

Chives Stir-Fried with Bean Sprouts

(CHING CHAU SUB CHOI)

清炒拾菜

I asked Ah Paw why this dish is called "ten vegetables" when I could only see two. This is how she explained it. The recipe's name translates literally as "Lightly Stir-Fried Ten Vegetables," but the word for chives is *gau choi*, which means "nine vegetables." Thus, nine vegetables plus bean sprouts equals ten. Was that clear? she asked. Of course.

4 cups cold water

¾ pound bean sprouts, washed, drained

2 tablespoons peanut oil

2 teaspoons minced ginger

1½ cups chives, washed, dried, about ⅛ inch of hard stems discarded, cut into 1-inch pieces

½ teaspoon salt

In a large pot, bring water to a boil over high heat. Place bean sprouts in water, stir no more than 10 seconds. Turn off heat, run cold water into pot and drain. Repeat, drain all excess water. Set aside. This should be done 1 hour before further preparation to ensure dryness. Occasionally loosen sprouts with chopstick, to help drying.

Heat wok over high heat for 1 minute. Add peanut oil, coat wok using spatula. When a wisp of white smoke appears, add ginger and stir. When ginger turns light brown, add chives, stir well, about 30 seconds, or until chives turn bright green. Add bean sprouts, stir well, cook for 1 minute. Turn off heat. Add salt and toss well to season. Transfer to heated dish, serve immediately.

SERVES 4 TO 6

Chives with Salted Pork

(Ham Chi Yuk Chau Gau Choi)

咸
猪
肉
炒
韭
菜

This is yet another use for that special salted pork. Chives grew in profusion, like the wild grasses they were, in my grandmother's garden, despite their "unholy" nature, as they do in mine. Their distinctive taste hints of both garlic and scallions. In Asian markets these days, they are often referred to as garlic chives.

SAUCE

3 tablespoons Chicken Stock (page 13)

¾ teaspoon cornstarch

1 teaspoon sesame oil

2½ tablespoons peanut oil

½ pound fresh chives, washed, hard ends trimmed, cut into 1-inch pieces

1½ cups Salted Pork (page 18) cut into slices 2 inches long, ½ inch wide, ¼ inch thick

1 tablespoon Shao-Hsing wine, or sherry

In a small bowl, combine all ingredients for sauce; reserve.

Heat wok over high heat 40 seconds. Add 1 tablespoon peanut oil, coat wok with spatula. When a wisp of white smoke appears, add chives, stir-fry for 1 minute, or until chives turn bright green. Turn off heat, remove from wok and reserve.

Wipe off wok and spatula with paper towels. Heat wok over high heat for 20 seconds. Add remaining peanut oil, coat wok. When a wisp of white smoke appears, add pork. Stir-fry for 1½ minutes. Drizzle wine into wok along its edges. Cook for 1 more minute, then add chives. Mix together about 1 minute until very hot. Make a well in the mixture, stir sauce, pour in and mix thoroughly. When sauce thickens, turn off heat, remove to a heated dish and serve immediately with cooked rice.

SERVES 4

Salted Pork and Tianjin Bok Choy Soup

(HAM JI YUK JIAN CHOY TONG)

咸
猪
肉
津
菜
湯

At virtually every lunch or dinner enjoyed at Ah Paw's table there was a soup served, simply because she liked them. Soups, clear and light, were her dishes of choice on those days when, as an observant Buddhist, she would eat no meat, poultry or fish. On other days her soups contained all manner of vegetables from her garden as well as meats, chicken and fish and seafood.

4 cups Chicken Stock (page 13)

1 slice ginger, ½ inch thick, lightly smashed

1 cup Salted Pork (page 18) cut into very thin 2½-inch slices

1¼ pounds Tianjin bok choy (Napa cabbage) washed, drained and cut into ¾-inch pieces on the diagonal, stalks and leaves separated

Place chicken stock and ginger in a large pot. Cover and bring to a boil over high heat. Add pork, stir and return to a boil. Add bok choy stalks, stir well and return again to a boil. Reduce heat to medium, cook for 1½ minutes. Raise heat to high, return to a boil. Add bok choy leaves, stir well and cook for 2 minutes or until tender. Taste and add salt if necessary. Transfer to a heated tureen and serve immediately.

SERVES 4 TO 6

Silk Squash Soup with Shredded Pork

(Sze Gua Tong)

This odd vegetable, a squash shaped like a zucchini, has ridges along its length. These must be pared off before the squash is prepared. This was a special treat at my grandmother's house because the squash was available only from late spring to early summer, less than two months a year. These days, silk squashes are available year-round in Asian markets. Select ones that are small and young.

MARINADE

2 teaspoons light soy sauce

2 tablespoons oyster sauce

1 teaspoon sesame oil

½ tablespoon Shao-Hsing wine, or sherry

1 teaspoon salt

1½ teaspoons sugar

2 teaspoons cornstarch

Pinch white pepper

2 pounds silk squash

2 tablespoons peanut oil

½ teaspoon salt

1 slice ginger, ½ inch thick, lightly smashed

4½ cups cold water

½ teaspoon baking soda

8 ounces lean pork butt, shredded

Combine all ingredients for marinade, add pork, toss, allow to rest 20 minutes.

Clean and wash squash and peel off ridges, but do not remove all of the green. Roll-cut squash: Starting at one end, cut diagonally into approximately ¾-inch slices. Turn squash one quarter turn between each cut. Reserve.

Heat wok over high heat for 40 seconds, add peanut oil, coat wok with spatula. When a wisp of white smoke appears add salt and ginger, stir for 15 seconds. When ginger browns, add squash, stir-fry until squash turns bright green, 2 to 3 minutes. Remove squash, place in large pot.

Add cold water and baking soda to pot and bring to a boil over high heat, uncovered. Lower heat and cook 3 to 4 minutes, or until squash softens. Raise heat to high, add pork and marinade. Separate pork shreds, bring back to a boil and cook over high heat, 2 minutes. Turn off heat, transfer to a heated tureen and serve immediately.

SERVES 4 TO 6

Bok Choy and Shredded Chicken Soup

(Bok Choy Gai See Tong)

Bok choy is perhaps the most familiar of Chinese vegetables. The bok choy I remember from my grandmother's garden was the sweetest, and most tender. This is not merely a rosy recollection; it truly was. In Ah Paw's kitchen bok choy was either stir-fried or made into soups. I was even taught how to blanch it and dry it in the sun, for later use in soups. This soup was one of my grandmother's favorites, a summer soup that she deemed cooling to the system.

MARINADE

1 tablespoon oyster sauce

1½ teaspoons light soy sauce

1 tablespoon Chinese white rice wine, or gin

1 teaspoon sesame oil

1 teaspoon sugar

¼ teaspoon salt

Pinch white pepper

2 teaspoons cornstarch

½ pound chicken cutlets, cut into 2½-inch julienne

4 cups Chicken Stock (page 13)

1 slice ginger, ½ inch thick, lightly smashed

1½ pounds bok choy, washed, dried well, cut into ½-inch pieces on the diagonal, stalks and leaves separated

2½ tablespoons Onion Oil (page 16)

Mix all ingredients for marinade in a bowl. Add chicken, toss and allow to rest 20 minutes.

Place chicken stock and ginger in a large pot, cover, bring to a boil over high heat. Add bok choy stalks, return to a boil. Lower heat to medium, cook for 5 to 7 minutes until stalks are tender. Raise heat back to high, add leaves, immerse thoroughly, stir and return to a boil. Add onion oil, stir, lower heat to medium. Cook 3 to 5 minutes, or until leaves are tender. Raise heat to high, add chicken and marinade, stir to mix thoroughly and allow to return to a boil. Boil soup for 1 minute. Taste for seasoning. Turn off heat, transfer to a heated tureen and serve immediately.

SERVES 4 TO 6

Broccoli Stir-Fried with Lop Cheung

(Yok Far Bun Lop Cheung)

玉
花
伴
腊
腸

This is a dish we usually ate during the month of the Lunar New Year. Though *lop cheung* (pork sausages) and *yun cheung* (pork liver sausages) are now available in Asian markets year-round, in my grandmother's time they were available only in the colder months. To eat them with broccoli (either the kind most familiar to Americans or Chinese broccoli; see page 41) was considered to be eating jade. In my kitchen I make this recipe with either one, though I often prefer to make it with the latter.

6 links Chinese sausage

1 2-pound bunch broccoli, florets cut off about 1½ inches from the top, washed and drained thoroughly for 45 minutes

2½ tablespoons peanut oil

1 slice ginger, ½ inch thick, lightly smashed

¾ teaspoon salt

1 tablespoon Chinese white rice wine, or gin

Steam sausages 20 minutes (see steaming directions, page 30). While sausages steam, cook the broccoli: Heat wok over high heat for 45 seconds. Add peanut oil and coat wok with spatula. When a wisp of white smoke appears, add ginger and salt, stir for 15 seconds, add broccoli, stir-fry 2 minutes. Drizzle wine into wok along its edges, cook for 2 minutes. This will create steam and broccoli will turn bright green.

When sausages are done, remove from steamer, cut into ⅛-inch diagonal slices. Place in a heated dish, surround with broccoli florets and serve immediately.

SERVES 4

Lantern Peppers Stir-Fried with Pork

(Dong Loon Jiu Chau Yuk See)

In Ah Paw's garden both red and green "lantern" peppers grew. These *dong loon jiu* were what are called bell peppers, but those in her garden were smaller and shaped quite like cylindrical lanterns. We steamed them, used them in stews, stuffed them, used them as garnishes for many dishes—but mostly we stir-fried them.

MARINADE

1½ tablespoons oyster sauce

1½ teaspoons sesame oil

2 teaspoons light soy sauce

¾ teaspoon ginger juice, mixed with 2 teaspoons Chinese white rice wine, or gin

2 teaspoons cornstarch

Pinch white pepper

1 teaspoon sugar

⅛ teaspoon salt

¾ pound fresh, lean pork loin, cut in half lengthwise, each half cut into slices ½-inch across

SAUCE

1½ tablespoons oyster sauce

1½ teaspoons light soy sauce

1 teaspoon sesame oil

⅛ teaspoon salt

1 teaspoon sugar

Pinch white pepper

1 tablespoon cornstarch

2 teaspoons Chinese white rice wine, or gin

½ cup Chicken Stock (page 13)

3½ tablespoons peanut oil

1 tablespoon minced ginger

¼ teaspoon salt

½ cup scallions, white portions only, julienned

¾ cup carrots (1 medium carrot), julienned

¼ cup water chestnuts, julienned

1¼ cups green bell peppers, julienned

2 teaspoons minced garlic

1 tablespoon Chinese white rice wine, or gin

Mix all ingredients for marinade. Add pork to it and allow to rest at least 20 minutes.

Mix all ingredients for sauce; reserve.

Heat wok over high heat for 40 seconds. Add 1½ tablespoons peanut oil, coat wok with spatula. When a wisp of white smoke appears, add ginger and salt and stir 20 seconds. Add scallions, stir, mix. Add carrots, stir and cook 20 seconds. Add water chestnuts, stir and cook 30 seconds. Add green peppers, stir. When peppers turn light green, 1 to 1½ minutes, turn off heat. Remove contents of wok to a dish and reserve.

Wipe off wok and spatula. Heat wok over high heat for 30 seconds. Add remaining 2 tablespoons peanut oil, coat wok. When a wisp of white smoke appears, add garlic and stir. When garlic releases its fragrance, about 20 seconds, add pork and marinade. Spread in a thin layer and tip wok side to side to ensure uniform cooking, until edges of slices turn white. Turn pork over, mix, add wine and cook until slices turn white. Add reserved vegetables, mix well and cook for 1½ minutes. Make a well in the mixture, stir sauce, pour in and mix thoroughly. When sauce thickens and bubbles, turn off heat, transfer to a heated dish and serve immediately with cooked rice.

SERVES 4 TO 6

WISDOM IN A BATCH OF BAD RICE

Even as I continued to learn to cook in my grandmother's kitchen, with the foods of garden and market, my education in other matters deepened. Aspects of life were transmitted to me by Ah Paw in stories, adages and morality tales. Some of these I had heard from my mother, of course, but after all it was my grandmother who had taught her daughter first, so why not tell them to her granddaughter, too? A favorite of hers had to do with a new bride who, despite the fact that she did not know how to cook well, was nevertheless required to cook rice for her new mother-in-law. What emerged from her earnest effort was a pot of rice, half of which was not cooked completely, the other half burned.

When she presented her effort to her mother-in-law, her husband quickly leaped to her defense. Before his mother could comment on his new wife's efforts, he remarked on how nicely crisped the uncooked rice was, how perfectly fragrant was that which had burned.

Ah Paw would tell me that a bride surely should not have to depend upon her husband to lie for her, but on the other hand the new bride's poor cooking effort had been a good test of faith for her new husband. Listen to what I have said, Ah Paw would tell me. I listened.

FOUR

FROM POND AND RIVER

地塘河流

FISH WAS OF THE UTMOST IMPORTANCE in my grandmother's house, both as food and as philosophy. She preferred to eat fish as often as possible for she deemed it easily digestible, and because it symbolized peace and serenity to her. In her salon there hung on one wall a red cloth with black calligraphy that read, *Man Shi Yue Ee*, or "A million things are peaceful and agreeable." The word *yue*, in the middle of the saying, is the word for fish. This wall hanging in the name of peace was on display year after year, put up just before the New Year and left there until it was replaced with an identical cloth at the same time the year following.

As part of her holdings, Ah Paw had a series of large freshwater ponds, in which fish were raised by the Chan family, who also saw to her gardens and orchards. From these ponds came all manner of carp, a sweet fish, as well as dace and catfish. The fish were well-fed with cut soft field grasses and sugarcane leaves, as well as the mash that remained after peanuts had been crushed for their oil.

Some fish was cooked virtually every day in my grandmother's kitchen, either steamed, in congees or soups or occasionally lightly fried, with Ah Paw ordering them by age, weight and size.

One day it might be a *wan yue*, the big-scaled golden-orange grass carp. On another day Ah Paw might fancy *soh yue*, the silver carp with its glittering shiny scales and small head, or its big-headed cousin, *dai tau yue*. Her ponds also held dace, *lang yue*, a smaller sweet fish usually used to mince into fish balls, and catfish, called *bak fu yue*, or "grand uncle fish" because of its long whiskers.

Dace lent itself to special dishes, one in particular that my grandmother's older servant, Sau Lin, cooked expertly. She would take a whole fish, cut along its stomach, remove its intestines, then carefully remove all its meat and bones, leaving the skin intact. The meat would be finely minced into a paste with dried shrimp, scallions, crushed peanuts, soy sauce, egg and coriander, then stuffed back into the skin so it resembled a whole fish. Then the fish would be pan-fried. It was a marvelous dish.

My grandmother preferred her fish steamed because it was so natural, but she was pleased with fish of any sort. She would say repeatedly, *"Yue ho ho sik,"* or "Fish tastes so very good," and, *"Ho yeung yee siu far,"* or "It is so easy to digest."

Most afternoons I would go out to the ponds, which sat amid the sugarcane fields and mulberry bushes of my grandmother's, and feed the fish. Often in the spring, in the time of heaviest rains, the ponds would overflow and the fish that had been raised would flow away, usually into the river, several branches of which flowed through Sah Gau, and quite often we would find pond-raised fish swimming in our river, mixing in with a porgielike flat fish, *jik yue hau*, distinguished by its rather delicate mouth. In fact, if a young woman had a beautiful mouth, she was said to have a *jik yue choi*. I say this of my granddaughter, Siu Siu, who has an exceptionally small and pretty mouth.

The river also yielded shrimp, which we would catch in small woven bamboo baskets. We would eat them in a variety of ways, feed them to Ah Paw's mynah or use them as bait. Our river also was home to a fish we called snakehead, a dense-fleshed fish very much like a striped bass, as well as live water snakes.

To be sure, fish of many varieties, including those that swam in saltwater, were available in the Sah Gau market, where we also bought clams, oysters and mussels. The flat fish of the sea, *lung lei*, or "dragon tongue," that was so highly prized in our market came from the waters off Jung Shan Yuen, a large rural district quite like Sun Tak Yuen, that was famed for being the birthplace of Sun Yat Sen, generally regarded as China's first revolutionary, who led his country out of Imperial rule into the modern world. It seemed only right that a great fish should come from the same place. That fish would occasionally find its way to the Sah Gau market, where it was sometimes sold live and was always snapped up fast.

So there was no lack of seafood in my grandmother's kitchen. As I noted earlier, one of the first dishes she taught me to make was steaming a piece of grass carp. Preparing more dishes with fish and other foods of the water followed. To this day, not a week goes by that I do not cook fish several times for my family and, when she is with me, for my granddaughter.

Baked Grass Carp

(Guk Wan Yue)

The grass carp was my grandmother's fish of choice. When young and small, it has many bones, but as it grows it becomes large and fleshy. It often grew so large that what was cooked was usually a fat, meaty center section of the fish, with the head reserved for casseroles and soups. Many people, myself included, prefer the tail portion, because there is less fat in its meat. To this day that is my preference. We ate grass carp most often cooked in a wok atop Ah Paw's stove, covered, so that in effect it was baked, even though she had no oven. It was delicious cooked this way, though we ate it also in soups, steamed it, braised it and pan-fried it.

Farm-raised grass carp can be found live in Asian markets. The best size is from 6 to 8 pounds, and should be asked for by its name. The fishmonger will have cut the fish in half, lengthwise, cleaned it, and will present it in its two pieces. As recommended, a meaty wedge of the center of the fish can be bought, skin on one side, flesh and bone on the other. I prefer a piece with the bone in, 1½ to 2 pounds. The fishmonger will already have scaled the fish and removed the intestines.

This recipe, a descendant from my grandmother's kitchen, is modified only by the fact that I truly bake it in an oven. Other than that, it is identical, including the use of ketchup, which serves the same coloring purpose as the traditional Chinese *keh chap*.

1½ pounds grass carp, middle portion

MARINADE

1 teaspoon Chinese white rice vinegar, or distilled white vinegar

1 tablespoon Chinese white rice wine, or gin

1 tablespoon light soy sauce

1 tablespoon peanut oil

½ teaspoon salt

⅛ teaspoon white pepper

1 tablespoon minced Chinese bacon or uncooked American-style bacon

2 tablespoons egg whites, beaten

4½ tablespoons ketchup

2 teaspoons minced garlic

1 tablespoon minced ginger

2 tablespoons scallions, finely sliced

3 tablespoons onions, minced

1 teaspoon sugar

2 tablespoons Chicken Stock (page 13)

Heat oven to 400 degrees F.

Wash fish thoroughly. Cut 3 slits in skin, side of fish to the backbone; do not cut through. Place in an ovenproof glass dish. Mix marinade, pour over the fish and rub well into the flesh on both sides. Allow to rest for 10 minutes. Mix sauce, pour over fish and rub into flesh and into the slits by hand, until well coated.

Place fish, slit side up, in oven and bake for 25 minutes, until fish flesh turns white. Test by gently pushing a chopstick into flesh. If it goes in easily, the fish is done. Remove from oven and serve in the baking dish, spooning sauce over each portion. The fish is best served with cooked rice, to enjoy the sauce.

SERVES 4 TO 6

Grass Carp with Fresh Tomatoes

(Fon Keh Ju Wan Yue)

What made this recipe so special was that we cooked it with the wild tomatoes that grew around the perimeter of Ah Paw's walled garden.

MARINADE

2 teaspoons Chinese white rice vinegar, or distilled white vinegar

1 tablespoon Chinese white rice wine, or gin

½ teaspoon salt

Pinch white pepper

SAUCE

1½ tablespoons oyster sauce

1 teaspoon salt

1 tablespoon sugar

1½ teaspoons sesame oil

2 tablespoons Chinese white rice wine, or gin

Pinch white pepper

2 teaspoons dark soy sauce

1½ tablespoons cornstarch

6 tablespoons Chicken Stock (page 13)

1½ grass carp, middle portion

5 tablespoons peanut oil

2 slices fresh ginger, each ½ inch thick

2 teaspoons minced ginger

2 teaspoons minced garlic

1½ pounds fresh tomatoes, washed, dried, cut into ½-inch cubes

2 scallions, trimmed, finely sliced

Mix marinade, reserve. Mix sauce, reserve.

Wash fish. Clean thoroughly and dry. Make two cuts into the center of the skin side of the fish to the bone; do not cut through. Place fish in a dish, add marinade, rub into the fish. Allow to rest 10 minutes.

Dry fish with paper towels. Heat wok over high heat for 40 seconds. Add 3 tablespoons peanut oil and 1 slice of ginger and coat wok with spatula. When a wisp of white smoke appears, place fish in wok. Lower heat, pan-fry for 3 minutes. Turn fish over, add second slice of ginger, fry for 5 minutes more, until fish begins to turn white. Remove fish from wok and set aside. Turn off heat. Discard ginger slices.

Empty oil from wok. Wipe off wok and spatula. Heat wok over high heat 40 seconds. Add remaining 2 tablespoons peanut oil. When a wisp of white smoke appears, add minced ginger and garlic, stir. When garlic turns light brown, add tomatoes. Stir for 1 minute, lower heat and cook for 5 minutes until tomatoes soften. Add sauce, stir together, bring to a boil. Return fish to the wok. Lower heat to medium. Spoon tomato mixture over fish, allow to simmer for 3 minutes. Turn off heat, add scallions and mix gently. Transfer fish to a heated dish, served immediately with cooked rice.

SERVES 4 TO 6

Fish and Lettuce Soup

(Sahng Choi Yue Pin Tong)

生菜魚片湯

This soup is adaptable to different fish. In my grandmother's kitchen it was made from either grass carp or silver carp, but its taste is quite good with striped bass, halibut, flounder, sole or sea bass as well. If grass carp is the choice, use the filleted back portion of the fish; for other fish use similar meaty filets.

MARINADE

½ teaspoon salt

1 teaspoon sugar

1½ teaspoons sesame oil

1 teaspoon cornstarch

1 teaspoon ginger juice mixed with 1 teaspoon Chinese white rice wine, or gin

1½ teaspoons light soy sauce

Pinch white pepper

12 ounces fresh grass carp, thinly sliced

4½ cups Chicken Stock (page 13)

1 slice ginger, ½ inch thick, lightly smashed

1 head iceberg lettuce, tough outer leaves discarded, washed, drained well and shredded (yields 7 cups, tightly packed)

2 tablespoons Scallion Oil (page 16)

Mix all ingredients for marinade. Place fish in a bowl, pour marinade over, mix to cover and allow to rest 10 minutes.

Place stock and ginger in a pot, bring to a boil over high heat. Add lettuce, stir and return to a boil. Add fish and marinade, stir, bring to a boil. Turn off heat, add scallion oil and stir. Transfer to a heated tureen and serve immediately.

SERVES 4 TO 6

Dragon Tongue Fish

(Soh Jah Lung Lei)

My grandmother looked forward to this special treat. As a rule she did not prefer her fish to be fried, but even she enjoyed this crisply fried sea fish. It was always made with the flat, sole-like lung lei. Only a sea fish would do, Ah Paw would decree, because of its taste. It derives its "dragon tongue" name from its tongue-like shape, wide, flat and thin. The way it was, and is, prepared is singular, deep-fried thoroughly, so crisp that even its small fins and tail bones are crisp, like chips, and edible. I find sole to be best for this recipe, but flounder will also do nicely.

1 sole, 1¼ pounds, scales, gills and intestines removed

MARINADE

1½ tablespoons Chinese white rice wine, or gin

1¼ teaspoons salt

1½ teaspoons Chinese white rice vinegar, or distilled white vinegar

⅛ teaspoon white pepper

6 cups peanut oil

1 extra-large egg, beaten

¾ cup flour

2 tablespoons scallions, trimmed and finely sliced

Wash fish thoroughly, dry with paper towels. Place in a large dish.

Combine all ingredients for marinade and pour over fish. Rub in to coat well, allow to rest 15 minutes.

Dry fish with paper towels. Heat wok over high heat for 1 minute, add peanut oil and heat to 375 degrees F. As oil heats, coat fish with beaten egg. Spread flour on sheet of waxed paper, dredge fish in it to coat thoroughly and shake off excess.

Place on a Chinese strainer, lower into the oil. Deep-fry for 3 minutes. Reduce heat, allowing oil temperature to lower to 350 degrees F. Fry for another 4 to 6 minutes, until fish turns light brown. If fish is too large to be totally covered with oil, ladle oil over it. If temperature is carefully regulated, fish will not burn. Turn off heat, place fish in strainer and drain over a large bowl. Allow fish to return to room temperature.

Reheat oil to 350 degrees F. Place fish in strainer back in oil and deep-fry for another 5 to 7 minutes, or until fish is golden brown and very crisp. Turn off heat, allow fish to drain over large bowl, at least 1 minute. Transfer to a heated platter, sprinkle with scallions and serve immediately.

SERVES 4

White-Boiled Shrimp

(Bok Chuk Har)

白灼蝦

This favorite of both my family and that of my grandmother is called "white-boiled" simply to denote that it is cooked unadorned, and that its flavor depends upon the quality of the live shrimp from which it is made. We ate these sweet river shrimp naturally, as they were boiled, with only the added taste of a simple dip to enhance their flavor. These days live shrimp are not a rarity, and are widely available in Asian markets as well as quality fishmongers. Live shrimp do not have to be deveined; they are naturally clean.

3 cups cold water

1 pound large (about 20 to 22 per pound) live shrimp

In a large pot, bring water to a rolling boil. Add shrimp, cover immediately, return to boil and boil shrimp for 1 minute. Turn off heat, leave pot cover on and allow shrimp to rest in water for 4 to 5 minutes, until shrimp curl.

Remove shrimp from pot with a strainer, place in a heated dish and serve. To eat, twist off head, remove shell and eat with dipping sauce.

SERVES 4

Dipping Sauce

2 teaspoons minced chili peppers

2 tablespoons light soy sauce

1 tablespoon Scallion Oil (page 16)

3 tablespoons Chicken Stock (page 13)

2 tablespoons scallions, finely sliced

Mix all sauce ingredients well, divide into 4 small soy sauce dishes and serve with shrimp.

N O T E   Shrimp that have been frozen, but not cooked, may be used in place of live shrimp. Those frozen are usually headless, and the recipe weight will be ¾ pound.

Shrimp that come with their backs already split and veins removed are known as easy-peel. Those still containing veins must be squeezed to remove the veins. The frozen shrimp are boiled for 1 minute as well, but should sit in the water for only 2 to 3 minutes.

Shrimp Stir-Fried in Bean Sauce

(Yuen See Chau Har)

原
鼓
炒
蝦

It is the sauce from the market that made this dish so special. The brown bean sauce is made from the soy beans found at the bottoms of the crocks in which soy sauce has been fermented and poured off. These beans, ground and pureed, were sold as sauce in the Sah Gau market. Today this sauce is jarred, often labeled Brown Bean Sauce, but just as often, Bean Sauce. There is no difference.

MARINADE

2 teaspoons dark soy sauce

2 tablespoons oyster sauce

1 teaspoon sesame oil

1½ teaspoons sugar

½ teaspoon grated ginger

2 teaspoons Chinese white rice wine, or gin

1¼ pounds extra large (about 32 to 36 per pound) fresh shrimp, heads removed, shelled, deveined, washed, dried

2½ tablespoons peanut oil

1½ teaspoons minced ginger

1 tablespoon bean sauce

1 tablespoon Chinese white rice wine, or gin

2 scallions, finely sliced

Mix all ingredients for marinade in a large bowl. Add shrimp, mix to coat and allow to rest 30 minutes. Drain through a strainer, reserve marinade.

Heat wok over high heat for 45 seconds. Add peanut oil, coat wok with spatula. When a wisp of white smoke appears, add minced ginger and stir. Add bean sauce and stir. Add shrimp and spread in a thin layer, tipping wok from side to side to spread heat evenly. Turn over. Drizzle wine into wok around its edges. Toss mixture together. If the mix is too dry, add a bit of the reserved marinade. When shrimp turn pink, turn off heat, add scallions and toss to mix. Remove from wok, transfer to a heated dish and serve with cooked rice.

SERVES 4 TO 6

N O T E   These may be served cool or at room temperature as an appetizer. Refrigerate, covered with plastic wrap, until ready to serve.

Shrimp Filling

(HAR HOM)

This is a most versatile preparation. In my grandmother's house it was used to stuff vegetables, bean curd and various dim sum. We also ate it cooked, as small shrimp pancakes or patties. We even ate it as a leftover, sliced and stir-fried with different vegetables, or added to soups. As with other fillings, because there was no refrigeration, this was prepared and eaten in the cooler winter months only. With refrigeration it can be made anytime and, once made, and allowed to rest, refrigerated, for at least four hours, or overnight. Prepared this way, it has an elegance and delicacy of flavor that complements other foods beautifully. It is important to use gray, or white, uncooked shrimp when preparing this filling, rather than pink uncooked shrimp. The grays hold together quite well; the pinks tend to fall apart.

1 pound uncooked gray shrimp, shelled, deveined, washed, dried, quartered and chopped into a fine paste

¾ teaspoon salt

1½ teaspoons sugar

¼ cup bamboo shoots, cut into ⅛-inch dice

2 scallions, trimmed, finely sliced

1½ tablespoons egg whites, beaten

2 teaspoons oyster sauce

1 teaspoon sesame oil

2 teaspoons Chinese white rice wine, or gin

⅛ teaspoon white pepper

Combine all ingredients well. Using a large bowl, pick up the mixture and throw it with some force against the side of the bowl. Repeat 5 or 6 times. (This will make the mixture firm. This technique I learned before I was 10 years old, and it serves me perfectly to this day.)

Place mixture in a shallow bowl, refrigerate for at least 4 hours, or overnight, covered.

Stuffed Mushrooms

(Bok Far Siu Mai)

百花燒賣

1 recipe Steamed Black Mushrooms (page 32), 24 pieces

Tapioca flour, for dusting

1 recipe Shrimp Filling (page 91)

6 tablespoons peanut oil, optional

Dust the cavity of the cap of each mushroom with tapioca flour, to bind the filling to the mushroom. Pack each mushroom with 1 to 1½ tablespoons of shrimp filling. With your finger, smooth the filling, and gently press it down to make certain it will not fall out.

Steam mushrooms for 6 minutes, or until shrimp turns pink. Serve immediately. (See steaming directions, page 30.)

TO PAN-FRY: Heat a cast-iron skillet over high heat for 1 minute. Add 3 tablespoons peanut oil to cover bottom of pan. When a wisp of white smoke appears, lower heat to medium and add mushrooms to pan, filling sides down. Fry 4 to 5 minutes until golden brown, turn and fry for another 3 minutes until done. If oil is absorbed you may need to add another tablespoon of peanut oil to pan. It is best to fry in 2 batches. Repeat process with second batch. Place first batch in a serving dish in a warm oven as second batch is pan-fried. Drain and serve immediately.

MAKES 24 MUSHROOMS

Pepper Siu Mai

(Lah Chiu Siu Mai)

2 medium red bell peppers

Tapioca flour, for dusting

1 recipe Shrimp Filling (page 91)

4½ tablespoons peanut oil (if pan-fried)

Wash, dry and seed peppers. Cut lengthwise into quarters and remove membranes. Cut each quarter in half, across, to make 16 pieces.

Dust cavity of each pepper section with tapioca flour. Divide filling into 16 equal portions. Using a butter knife, press one portion of filling into each pepper cavity, pressing firmly.

Stuffed pepper can be either steamed or pan-fried. Steam for 6 minutes over medium heat. (See steaming directions, page 30.) Serve immediately.

TO PAN-FRY: Heat a large cast-iron skillet over high heat for 1 minute. Add 3 tablespoons peanut oil to cover bottom. When a wisp of white smoke appears, lower heat to medium and place all 16 stuffed pepper sections in pan, stuffed side down. Fry for 4 minutes, until filling is golden brown. Turn over, fry for 3 minutes more, until done. If oil is absorbed, it may be necessary to add the remaining 1½ tablespoons of oil. Turn off heat, transfer to a heated dish and serve immediately.

MAKES 16 STUFFED PEPPERS

Stuffed Bitter Melon

(Yueng Fu Guah)

Bitter melon is widely regarded as a curative food. It has a mildly bitter taste, but is not unpleasant. Eaten alone, pan-fried or stir-fried, my grandmother believed it could combat diabetes. She also used it often as an infusion to make tea for diabetics.

1 recipe Shrimp Filling (page 91)

S A U C E

2 tablespoons oyster sauce

2 teaspoons light soy sauce

½ teaspoon salt

1 teaspoon sugar

1 tablespoon Shao-Hsing wine, or sherry

1½ teaspoons sesame oil

Pinch white pepper

1½ tablespoons cornstarch

¾ cup Chicken Stock (page 13)

3 medium-sized (2½ pounds) bitter melons, washed, dried, both ends discarded, cut into 1¼-inch sections across and center pulp removed, to make 18 pieces

Tapioca flour, for dusting

5 to 6 tablespoons peanut oil

2½ tablespoons fermented black beans, washed and drained

3 cloves garlic, coarsely chopped

3 tablespoons coriander, finely sliced

Divide shrimp filling into 18 equal portions.

Mix all ingredients for sauce, reserve.

Dust cavity of each bitter melon round with tapioca flour. Stuff each round with equal portion of shrimp filling, to bulge out slightly on both sides. Continue until all rounds are stuffed, place on waxed paper and reserve.

Heat cast-iron skillet over high heat for 1 minute. Add 3 tablespoons peanut oil to cover bottom. When a wisp of white smoke appears, add stuffed melon rounds on one stuffed side. Lower heat to medium. Fry 3 minutes, turn over, fry for 4 minutes more until done. You may have to add additional oil to pan if oil is absorbed. Remove cooked rounds, reserve.

Raise heat to high. Make certain there is sufficient oil to cover bottom; if not add remaining oil. When a wisp of white smoke appears, add black beans and garlic, stir and cook until garlic releases its fragrance, about 15 seconds. Lower heat, stir sauce, pour in and mix well. Bring to a boil. When mixture bubbles, add melon rounds, lower heat and spoon sauce over the rounds. Cover pan and cook 3 to 4 minutes until melon rounds soften and become tender. Turn off heat, transfer to a heated dish, sprinkle with coriander and serve with cooked rice.

MAKES 18 PIECES

Stuffed Bean Curd

(Yung Dau Fu)

8 cakes fresh firm bean curd

Tapioca flour, for dusting

1 recipe Shrimp Filling (page 91)

7 tablespoons peanut oil, optional

Drain bean curd cakes over a bowl for 3 hours until thoroughly dry. Pat with paper towels to ensure dryness. Cut each cake in half, diagonally, and with a small pointed knife, cut out a pocket in the diagonal side. Dust each pocket with tapioca flour, then fill each with 1½ tablespoons of shrimp filling. Pack smoothly with flat side of knife.

Stuffed bean curd may either be steamed or pan-fried. Steam for 8 to 10 minutes, until shrimp filling turns pink. (See steaming directions, page 30.) Serve immediately.

TO PAN-FRY: Heat a cast-iron skillet over high heat for 1 minute. Add 3 tablespoons peanut oil to cover bottom. When a wisp of white smoke appears, lower heat to medium and place half of the bean curd sections in the pan, stuffed side down. Fry for 4 minutes until golden brown, turn over and fry for additional 2 minutes on each side. Add 1 to 1½ tablespoons peanut oil to pan, if needed. Repeat for second batch. Place first batch on serving plate in a warm oven as second batch is cooked. When done, drain and serve immediately.

Traditionally these are served with small dishes of soy sauce for dipping.

MAKES 16 PIECES

Lobster Steamed with Ginger

(Geung Chung Jing Lung Har)

In our family. lobster was a rare treat, reserved for holidays and family occasions, but also restricted by the season. It came to my grandmother's market only in the warmer summer months, usually from Guangzhou. The lobster was referred as *lung har*, or "dragon shrimp," because of its appearance. It was clawless, with a big tapering body, somewhat like a giant shrimp. It is still the lobster found in the waters off China and in most of Asia. The meat of these clawless lobsters, often three pounds or more, is as sweet as that of any lobster off the coasts of Maine or Canada. Oddly, when I was a girl, I would help to prepare it, but would never eat it, because I did not like its sweetness. But I really enjoyed chewing on the shells, a taste I still have.

For these recipes, I use the more familiar clawed lobster because it is readily available. Kill the lobster yourself by plunging a knife into the underside of its head, or have your fishmonger do it for you. Split it, and remove the inedible inner portion of the cavity.

MARINADE

2 tablespoons Chinese white rice wine, or gin

1 tablespoon light soy sauce

2 tablespoons Scallion Oil (page 16)

¼ teaspoon salt

1 teaspoon sugar

1½ teaspoons sesame oil

Pinch white pepper

1 teaspoon grated ginger

1 fresh 2-pound lobster

3 tablespoons shredded ginger

2 scallions, white portions only, cut into 1½-inch lengths, shredded

6 sprigs coriander

Mix all ingredients for marinade; set aside.

Prepare lobster: With a cleaver, cut the head and claws off the lobster. Cut tail section into bite-size pieces. Similarly, cut claws and head into pieces. Place lobster pieces in a bowl, pour marinade over, mix to coat and allow to rest 30 minutes.

Place lobster pieces in a steamproof dish and pour marinade over top. Sprinkle shredded ginger and scallions over lobster and steam 12 to 15 minutes, or until lobster shells turn red, meat turns white. (See steaming directions, page 30.) Do not oversteam or the lobster will be tough. When done, remove from steamer, garnish with coriander and serve with cooked rice.

SERVES 4

Wok-Baked Rice Wine Lobster

(Hua Tiao Guk Lung Har)

花
雕
焗
龍
蝦

This recipe, which is quite old, is a true heirloom. Not only was the lobster a treat, but so was its flavor, that of a very special Shao-Hsing wine, Hua Tiao, which in my grandmother's dialect was called Far Diu. The customary rice-based Shao-Shing wine is, in terms of aroma and taste, very much like a medium dry sherry. Hua Tiao, or Far Diu, is far more subtle. Its aroma is floral, and the taste is far more smooth and elegant. To be sure, both satisfy the cooking dictum once given me by my father, who said that when it came to wine, if it could not be drunk and enjoyed, it should not be used for cooking. These days Hua Tiao is widely available in Asian markets and wine shops that stock Chinese wines. This special Hua Tiao wine was, in my grandmother's time, sold in brown crockery gourdlike jugs. These days it is brown glass bottles labeled usually *"Shao-Hsing Hua Tiao Chiew,"* which translates simply as "Shao-Hsing Hua Tiao Wine." If it is unavailable, I suggest that Cognac be used instead, because of its elegance.

This preparation, in addition to its special flavor, illustrates the versatility of the wok, in its role as a temporary oven.

MARINADE

1 teaspoon ginger juice mixed with 2 tablespoons Hua Tiao wine, or Cognac

1½ tablespoons light soy sauce

2 tablespoons oyster sauce

½ teaspoon salt

2 teaspoons sugar

Pinch white pepper

1 tablespoon sesame oil

1 2-pound lobster, split, inedible cavity portions removed

3 tablespoons peanut oil

2 tablespoons shredded ginger

2 scallions, trimmed, cut into ½-inch sections on the diagonal, white and green portions separated

2 cloves garlic, minced

1½ tablespoons Hua Tiao wine, or Cognac

1 teaspoon cornstarch

Mix marinade ingredients together and reserve.

Prepare lobster: With a cleaver, cut off head and claws. Cut tail section into bite-size pieces. Similarly, cut claws and head into pieces. Place lobster pieces in a bowl, pour marinade over, mix to coat, allow to rest 20 minutes. Remove lobster from marinade, reserve. Reserve marinade.

Heat wok over high heat for 1 minute. Add peanut oil, coat wok with spatula. When a wisp of white smoke appears, add shredded ginger and white portions of scallions, stir 10 seconds. Add garlic. When garlic turns light brown, about 8 seconds, add lobster pieces. Spread in a single layer and cook for 1 minute. Stir all ingredients well for 2 minutes. Drizzle wine into wok along its edges and mix well, for 1 minute. Add green portions of scallions, stir briefly. Add half of reserved marinade, mix well.

Cover wok with a wok cover, cook for about 4 minutes, or until lobster shells turn red and meat whitens. Stir cornstarch into remaining marinade, pour into wok. Stir until sauce thickens. Turn off heat, transfer to a heated dish and serve immediately with cooked rice.

SERVES 4

Clams with Black Beans

(See Jop Chau Hin)

To us, clams were continual reminders of a prosperous life. When they opened after boiling, they resembled vaguely the gold coins of past ages. Ah Paw, who loved steamed clams, would remind me as she ate that clams were one of those shellfish declared acceptable for Buddhist vegetarians. This classic recipe, which I cooked first in my grandmother's kitchen, and which I now cook in my own, has not changed one bit.

SAUCE

2 tablespoons oyster sauce

1 teaspoon dark soy sauce

1 teaspoon sesame oil

1 tablespoon Shao-Hsing wine, or sherry

¾ teaspoon sugar

1 tablespoon cornstarch

Pinch white pepper

5 ounces Vegetable Stock (page 14)

8 cups water

30 medium-sized clams, scrubbed to remove dirt and sand

3 tablespoons peanut oil

1 tablespoon shredded ginger

1 tablespoon shredded garlic

2 teaspoons fermented black beans, washed and drained

2 tablespoons scallions, white portions, finely sliced

Mix all ingredients for sauce, reserve.

Bring 8 cups of water to a boil in a large pot. Add clams, bring back to a boil and cook, about 4 minutes. Move clams around with a wooden spoon as they boil. They will begin to open. As they do, remove with a slotted spoon to a waiting dish. This should be done promptly or they will toughen. Continue process until all clams open.

Heat wok over high heat for 40 seconds. Add peanut oil and coat wok with spatula. Add ginger, garlic and black beans, stir and mix until the garlic and black beans release their fragrances, 1 to 2 minutes. Add clams, stir and mix for 2 minutes. Make a well in the center of the clams, stir sauce, pour in. Stir continually until sauce thickens and clams are thoroughly coated, about 1 minute. Turn off heat, transfer to a heated serving dish, sprinkle scallions on top and serve immediately.

SERVES 4 TO 6

Mussel and Noodle Soup

(Hok Hin Mai Fun Tong)

Traditionally the mussels used in soups were dried. They were initially sold loose in market shops, later in packages. An advantage of dried mussels, when reconstituted by soaking in water, was an intense, assertive flavor. However, they also tended to be tough. As a young girl I made this soup with dried mussels and vegetables, without noodles. In my own kitchen today I prefer fresh, shelled mussels, with vegetables and noodles, for the richness and subtlety of their combined flavors.

2 quarts water

1 slice ginger, 1 inch thick, lightly smashed

1¼ teaspoons salt

1 teaspoon Chinese white rice vinegar, or distilled white vinegar

1½ pounds mussels in shells, scrubbed with a hard brush to remove sand and beards, rinsed well

4 cups Vegetable Stock (page 14)

1 tablespoon soy sauce

2 tablespoons Shao-Hsing wine, or sherry

2 teaspoons Scallion Oil (page 16)

4 ounces snow peas, halved on the diagonal ends, strings removed

¼ cup scallions, white portions only, finely sliced

8 ounces dried rice noodles, ¼ inch wide (linguine), soaked in hot water 20 to 30 minutes, until pliable, drained and loosened with chopsticks

2 tablespoons coriander, finely sliced

In a large pot place water, ginger, 1 teaspoon salt and vinegar. Cover and bring to a boil over high heat for 1 minute. Add mussels. As they open, remove them from the pot to a bowl and reserve.

Place vegetable stock in a large pot. Add the remaining ¼ teaspoon salt, soy sauce, wine and scallion oil. Cover and bring to a boil over high heat. Add snow peas and scallions and allow to return to a boil. Add noodles, allow to return to a boil. Turn off heat immediately, add reserved mussels and stir well. Transfer to individual soup bowls, sprinkle with coriander and serve immediately.

SERVES 4 TO 6

NOTE If dried rice noodles are unavailable, use dried linguine pasta, and boil just until al dente.

MISADVENTURES OF A MUD GIRL

One of my favorite pastimes when I visited Ah Paw's house was feeding her fish, and I came to regard some of them, as they grew, as pets. I would bring handfuls of fresh grasses and cups of dried peanut mash and throw them into the ponds, enjoying the fish spurting to the pond's surface, their mouths opening and closing as they fed. I also liked to be with the Chans in October, when they would drain individual ponds, remove fully grown fish to be taken to the market or be eaten, and to transfer small fish to other ponds.

I became so confident around these ponds that one day I became careless. As the Chans were standing in the drained pond mud handing fish up and out, I tried to grab a grass carp that I thought I knew. I fell into the mud and found myself covered from my hair to my sandals. The Chan boys thought this was terribly funny and laughed as Mr. Chan lifted me out of the mud, telling me, "*Nei gum yat sik jai*," "Today you will eat no fish, you are a vegetarian."

I washed off as much mud as I could with water from the field buckets, then made my way to my grandmother's house, tiptoed past her salon so she would not see or hear me and picked up a change of clothing. I went off to one of her empty houses, bathed the remainder of the mud off myself, then came back to Ah Paw's house and into her salon to wish her a good afternoon. She looked at me steadily for a long moment, then said, "*Ah Fei. Oh, Ah Fei.* Next time catch a fish. Do not let the fish catch you. You have become a *lai loi*." This translates as "mud girl."

At the time, I confess I was not amazed, for I believed that my Ah Paw simply knew all things. I found out later that my misadventure had been reported to her by one of the Chan boys. Yet I still thought she knew everything. Nor did she report my afternoon misfortune to those around that night's dinner table. When the steamed grass carp was served, Ah Paw smiled, sharing our secret. She said only, "This is Ah Fei's fish."

INTO THE LUNAR NEW YEAR

THE LUNAR NEW YEAR WAS THE most glorious time of the year for me as a young girl. Traditionally regarded throughout China as a time of rebirth and renewal, it was surely that for me, as well as a time for all sorts of special activities and observances, and all manner of foods and sweets. I looked forward to the days just before the New Year when I knew that I would receive a new red dress, new hair ornaments, stockings, undergarments and shoes. Then, after my sixth birthday, I knew that my new New Year's dress would no longer have to be red, but any color or pattern I fancied, because I was no longer considered to be a baby.

The occasion was twice as delicious for me because I helped celebrate in two houses, my own in Siu Lo Chun, and with Ah Paw in Sah Gau. In our house I would help my mother clean and dust, hang our calligraphic good luck sayings above our doorways, and replace our old picture of Tsao Chun, the Kitchen God, with a new image. When I was finished I would hurry to my grandmother's house, where the New Year preparations were far more elaborate.

It was, and still is, the most important time of the year in China for food. In my grandmother's kitchen there was cooking for ancestor offerings, later shared by the family. There were New Year's Eve banquets, and New Year's Day banquets, with care taken to cook and serve dishes of symbolism and New Year's significance. There was fashioning of special cakes to be served to visiting guests, and there were, of course, the regular meals to be cooked in the midst of this holiday, which lasts more than a month.

In Ah Paw's house, the New Year began symbolically on any day in the twelfth month deemed propitious, as determined by Ah Paw after she consulted her Tung Sing. This was an astrological book that she consulted at various times of the year in search of the more advantageous days for various observances. In this particular case it was to determine the proper date for *hoy yau wok*, or "open oil wok" day, on which to begin cooking for the New Year. This was largely a symbolic day, and simply meant that some food had to be deep-fried in a wok to formally open the New Year's cooking season. It was possible that no other cooking would be done for days, but the day had been set formally. Often, Ah Paw's servants would fry some lotus root chips or nuts.

Several days later I would go with my number-two aunt and my grandmother's servants to the Sah Gau community rice grinder to pulverize rice into the powder used for New Year's dumplings. We ground more than sixty pounds of rice, more than thirty-five pounds of which were glutinous rice, in a big stone bowl, pounding it with the flat of a heavy board that we worked like a seesaw. As the rice was ground, we would put it into bamboo trays and allow it to dry in the sun. By the end of our day we had sufficient rice flour for an entire year, and my legs had been well-exercised. This rice grinding day was also determined by Ah Paw and her Tung Sing.

That same book dictated the next step toward our New Year's celebration, the day of *soh chun*, or "brush dust," when every corner of the house, every ceiling beam, every piece of furniture was dusted. The chimney was cleared of soot, and the kitchen stoves were cleaned. Knives and scissors were put out of sight to ensure that the promise of continued good luck would not be broken. Then, just about a week before the New Year, all of the papers in Ah Paw's house with the slogans of good fortune and adages that she lived by, as well as the names and images of gods, were taken down and replaced with new ones.

One by one, the long red strips were taken down. *Man Shu Yue Ee*, "A Million Things Agreeable," *Sung Ee Hing Long*, "Good Business," *Lung Mah Jing Sun*, "Be

As Healthy As a Dragon and a Horse" and *Loh Siu Ping On*, "The Aged and Young Should Be Safe" all came down to be replaced by identical, freshly written signs. Above the door leading into the living room, and above the doors to both bedrooms, was written *Cheut Yap Ping On*, "Be Safe As You Go In and Out." In the living room that was my grandmother's salon and dining room, was an altar, on which were displayed etched sticks with the names of her ancestors as well as a paper image of Guan Gung, the God of Protection. In front of the altar, on the floor, was the image of Dei Jueh, Landlord of the Spirits, who was asked to bless Ah Paw's house. Opposite this altar, just outside the door, was another long strip of black on red calligraphy. *Tin Gun Chi Fook*, it read: "May the Goodness of Heaven Bring Wealth."

These were what my grandmother surrounded herself with, what she quoted often, what she lived by and were as important to her as the proper behavior set down in the Analects of Confucius, or the Buddhism she observed. The images of the Entrance God, Wei Chung, were replaced as well, as were those of the Door Gods—Shen Shu to the left, Yu Lei, to the right. The last of these messages to the gods to be attached to the walls of Ah Paw's house was always set above the front door jamb. It read *Ng Fook Lam Moon*, or "May the Five Gods of Fortune Arrive at Your Door."

This was also the day when the new image of the Kitchen God, Tsao Chun, was replaced. All of the old calligraphy had been taken down, and all the old images of the gods were placed in a pile. Atop the pile went the image of Tsao Chun, with honey smeared on his lips. The papers would be set afire, and as they burned and their ashes went skyward it was said that Tsao Chun had gone to Heaven to report only good things about the family with whom he had lived for the past year.

On this Kitchen God day his new image above the kitchen stoves would be honored with a small and simple dinner of white cut chicken and pork, and fresh oranges, tangerines, pomegranates and stalks of sugarcane, these used as incense burned before his image. He was honored with the fruits of the kitchen, three cups of rice wine, three cups of tea, three bowls of rice, and three pairs of chopsticks. All of this preparation ended about four days before the New Year, and then cooking for the holiday began in earnest.

Before cooking for ourselves, we cooked for any guests who might come calling, and as gifts for relatives, friends and neighbors. We made spongy steamed cakes, called *song goh*, from our ground rice flour, sugar and water; rice flour dumplings, called *yau kok*, filled with crushed peanuts, shredded coconut and sesame seeds; and my favorite, *jin dui*. These were balls of puffed rice mixed with sugarcane syrup, which the servants and I covered with thin layers of glutinous rice dough. I took great delight in molding them into the shapes of baby chicks and pomegranates before

The Kitchen God, Tsao Chun, in our household and that of my grandmother, was regarded as a benign spy. All year; from one Lunar New Year to the next, his image, on the wall in back of our stove, would look upon us to see how we behaved in the kitchen. We knew that just before the New Year he would go to Heaven and report on our family to the Jade Emperor.

We, of course, wished him to say only pleasant things about us to the emperor, so on the twenty-fourth day of the last month, a week before the New Year celebration, we would take his image down from the wall, smear his mouth with honey and then burn the image. We would see him rising Heavenward in the smoke and know only sweet tales would be coming from his lips.

In other households his mouth would be coated with sugar, with sweet pastries, often with wine for his journey up. But we thought honey was sufficient. Still other houses, not as trusting of the Kitchen God as we, would coat his lips with sweet sticky rice so he would not be able to even open them to make a report. This was rejected in our family, and I believed as a girl that good behavior would be rewarded with a happy report by Tsao Chun.

deep-frying them. These were especially earmarked for my young cousins and myself. The normal, round *jin dui*, about the size of a baseball, were reserved for elders. Also included in our annual New Year guest table was *lin goh*, a cake of steamed rice, yeast and water, sweetened with sugarcane sugar, which when sliced and served to a visitor was a wish that he or she who received it would experience a year better than the one before.

All of these confections took considerable time to make. Although they were usually available premade in the town market, Ah Paw would have none of that. *"Ho hoi sum,"* she would say, which indicated that there was joy to be found in the making. It is her message: enjoy the work, and learn, that I preach when teaching my students how to prepare dishes that require more than a little effort.

My grandmother insisted that these gifts of food be a family affair, with the servants, my number-two aunt and myself, sharing the effort. Here are some other gifts of food that we made in her kitchen in those exciting days leading to the New Year.

A CHINESE NEW YEAR FAMILY PORTRAIT TAKEN IN 1958.
STANDING LEFT TO RIGHT ARE MY COUSIN JOSEPHINE; MY NUMBER-SIX AUNT,
WITH WHOM I LIVED UNTIL I LEFT HONG KONG; ME; AND MY COUSIN CHRISTINA.
KNEELING IN FRONT ARE MY COUSINS SHIRLEY AND DAVID.

Turnip Cake

(Lor Bok Goh)

As with many foods at the New Year, this cake is at once nourishment and symbol. The cake, the goh, represents one's job, business, or fortune, and as the cake rises during cooking, one's position is said to improve. Noticeable in this recipe is the use of liquefied pork fat. This is traditional, but peanut oil can also be used.

1½ pounds (4½ cups, tightly packed) fresh Chinese turnips, peeled and coarsely grated

3¼ cups cold water

1 slice ginger, 1 inch thick, lightly smashed

3 tablespoons Chinese white rice wine, or gin

2 large cloves garlic, large, peeled and left whole

Pinch white pepper

10 ounces (2⅓ cups) rice flour

6 ounces (1½ cups) glutinous rice flour

2 cups plus 1 tablespoon cold water

⅓ cup liquefied pork fat, or peanut oil

2 tablespoons dried shrimp, soaked in water to soften, drained and cut into ¼-inch dice

3 Chinese sausages (*lop cheung*), cut into ¼-inch dice

½ cup Chinese bacon, cut into ¼-inch dice

⅛ teaspoon white pepper

3¾ teaspoons salt

3 tablespoons scallions, finely sliced (optional)

3 tablespoons coriander, finely sliced (optional)

Grease a 9-inch round, 3-inch-deep cake pan; set aside.

In a large pot, place the turnips, the 3¼ cups cold water, ginger, wine, garlic and white pepper. Cover and bring to a boil over high heat. Lower heat and simmer, with lid left open a little, for 10 minutes. Turn off heat, remove pot from stove, allow to cool, then discard ginger and garlic.

In large bowl mix rice flours with 2 cups and 1 tablespoon water. Add liquefied pork fat and mix well to combine. Add dried shrimp, sausages, bacon, white pepper and salt, and mix well to combine thoroughly. Add turnip mixture, including cooking liquid, to the bowl, and mix well to combine thoroughly.

Place the mixture in a greased 9-inch round cake pan. Place cake pan on a rack, add 8 cups boiling water in wok, cover, steam for 1 hour, 15 minutes. During the steaming process, add boiling water to the wok every 15 minutes. Test cake by inserting a chopstick. If the mixture does not stick to chopstick, it is done. Turn off heat. Allow to set 5 to 7 minutes. Remove cake pan from steamer, cut into portions and serve, sprinkled with finely sliced scallions and coriander, if desired.

N O T E   This cake was kept on hand for guests. It was always served hot. To heat, resteam for 5 to 7 minutes until hot. Slice and serve.

Pan-Fried Turnip Cake

(Jin Lor Bok Goh)

This most traditional preparation is a must for New Year visitors. Because my grandmother was a total vegetarian for the first fifteen days of the New Year, she did not eat this cake, but she insisted that it be on hand for visitors to her house. This pan-fried cake is quite different from the steamed version it is based on. Before pan-frying, the cake should be at room temperature. Whatever portion is to be used, the entire cake should be sliced into portions first, then pan-fried. Before pan-frying, slices should be cut from whole cake as needed. For the best taste, I recommend slices ½ inch thick by 2½ inches long.

> Peanut oil, as needed, to cover bottom of pan
>
> 1 steamed Turnip Cake (page 111), cut into portions
>
> 2 tablespoons scallions, finely sliced (optional)
>
> 2 tablespoons coriander, finely sliced (optional)

Pour sufficient oil to cover bottom of cast iron fry pan. Heat over high heat until a wisp of white smoke appears. Add turnip cake slices, lower heat. Pan-fry until light brown, about 3 minutes, turn over, fry for another 3 minutes. If oil is absorbed, add 1 to 2 tablespoons additional.

Drain slices on paper towels, serve immediately with sliced scallions and coriander, as desired.

Leftover turnip cake cannot be frozen. It should be refrigerated, but before pan-frying should be allowed to come to room temperature.

Taro Root Cake

(Wu Tau Goh)

This is another of those special New Year cakes. Essentially it's quite similar to turnip cake but made with the favored taro root, known for its purple-threaded texture. I remember asking Ah Paw about this cake before making it for the first time, and noting that its ingredients were similar. What is the difference, I asked her? "Ah Fei," she answered, "Ah Fei. I thought your name was Ah Fei. Perhaps it should be Chun Choi. One is made with turnips. One is made with taro." *Chun choi*, simply translated, means "dunderhead."

¾ pound taro root, skin and hard ends removed, cut into ½-inch dice, to yield 2 cups tightly packed

1¾ cups cold water

1 cup, 3 tablespoons rice flour

⅔ cup glutinous rice flour

1⅔ cups cold water

¼ cup liquefied pork fat, or peanut oil

2 Chinese sausages (*lop cheung*), cut into ¼-inch dice

¼ cup Chinese bacon, cut into ¼-inch dice

1½ tablespoons dried shrimp, soaked in water to soften, cut into ¼-inch dice

8 cups boiling water

3 tablespoons scallions, finely sliced

3 tablespoons coriander, finely sliced

Place taro and 1¾ cups cold water in a large pot, bring to a boil over high heat. Lower heat to simmer and cover, leaving a small opening and simmer 15 to 20 minutes, until taro is very tender. Turn off heat, allow to cool. As taro cools, grease an 8-inch-round cake pan and set aside.

In a large bowl mix rice flours and 1⅔ cups cold water. Add liquefied pork fat until well combined. Add sausage, bacon, shrimp and salt, and combine well. Add taro and its cooking liquid to the bowl, stir and mix to combine thoroughly. Pour into prepared cake pan.

Place 8 cups boiling water in wok and turn heat to high. Place cake pan on a rack in wok over boiling water, cover and steam, 1¼ hours. During steaming process, add boiling water to wok every 15 minutes. Insert a chopstick into the cake. If it comes out clean, cake is done. If not, steam for 15 minutes longer, then test again.

Turn off heat, allow cake to set 10 to 15 minutes in wok. Remove pan from wok. Leave cake in pan and cut into slices, serve, sprinkled with scallions and coriander, if desired.

To pan fry, follow instructions for pan-frying turnip cake (page 113).

Water Chestnut Cake

(Sang Maw Mah Tai Goh)

This simple dish is a New Year prize. Its sweet flavor is one of the recurring themes of the New Year. It was special to my grandmother, and it is to me as well. I make it not only every New Year, along with Turnip Cake, but also at other times throughout the year when I fancy it. The water chestnut powder at this recipe's base is cereal-like, and can be eaten as a breakfast porridge, when cooked with water and dark brown sugar. Among traditional Chinese it is considered a substitute for mothers' milk when cooked with water. My granddaughter, Siu Siu, loves it.

3¾ cups boiling water

1⅔ cups dark brown sugar

1¼ pounds (4½ cups) canned water chestnuts, drained and coarsely chopped

8 ounces water chestnut powder mixed with 1 cup cold water

Grease a 9-inch-square cake pan.

Pour boiling water into a wok over high heat, add sugar and stir to dissolve. Add chopped water chestnuts and mix well. Add water chestnut powder mixture. Turn heat under wok to low. Stir mixture continually in one direction for 5 to 7 minutes, until mix is very thick and pasty.

Pour water chestnut mixture into greased pan. Place pan on a rack in wok. Add 8 cups boiling water, cover and steam for 40 minutes until it sets firmly and becomes translucent. (See steaming directions, page 30.) Replenish boiling water after 20 minutes. Turn off heat, remove cake pan from steamer. Allow to set 4 minutes. Slice immediately and serve.

This is a most unusual cake. When freshly steamed, and sliced, it has the consistency of a firm jelly. As it cools, it becomes very much like an aspic. It can be frozen either whole, or in slices. To reheat, allow cake to return to room temperature, then steam for 10 minutes or until heated through. It will become more jellylike again. Eat it just as if it had been made fresh.

It can be pan-fried as well, but it must be cooled and refrigerated overnight preferably (not frozen) before doing so. To pan-fry, cut cooled cake into slices 2 inches square, ½ inch thick, and pan-fry in the same manner as turnip cake (page 113).

Scallion Pancakes

(Sahng Chung Bok Bang)

These thin scallion pancakes were usually served by my grandmother with afternoon tea—black, fermented bo lei tea, which she insisted was good for digestion. During the New Year time, these cakes were offered to guests, either with tea or with a small cup of pungent Chinese rice wine. The scallion pancakes themselves, I believe, were creations of her kitchen and are markedly different from those with which most people are familiar. I have never seen them in any restaurant. They are thin, crepelike, made from a bleached wheat flour batter and fried in an iron pan. I make them every New Year in my kitchen, in Ah Paw's memory.

1¼ cups bleached wheat flour

1½ teaspoons baking powder

1 medium egg, beaten

1½ cups, plus 2 to 4 tablespoons cold water

¾ teaspoon salt

Pinch white pepper

2 tablespoons dried shrimp, soaked in hot water to soften, then finely diced

⅓ cup Chinese bacon, finely diced

½ cup Chinese sausage (*lop cheung*), finely diced

7 scallions, trimmed, finely sliced

1½ tablespoons peanut oil, plus additional oil for pan, as needed

Mix flour and baking powder. Add egg and 1½ cups cold water and mix in one direction until smooth. Add salt and pepper, mix well. Add shrimp, bacon, sausages, scallions and peanut oil, blend thoroughly. The batter should be thin. If not, add 2 to 4 tablespoons of water.

Heat a crepe pan or a nonstick fry pan, add sufficient peanut oil to coat bottom. Pour about 3 tablespoons of batter into pan, cook 2 minutes, or until pancake sets. Turn over with spatula and cook until light brown. Remove from pan and place in a heated dish in an oven set at Warm. Repeat the process until 12 pancakes are cooked. You may need to add about 1 to 2 teaspoons oil to pan between pancakes. Keep regulating heat to avoid either overcooking or undercooking.

Serve with tea, as a snack or as a course of a larger meal.

MAKES 12 PANCAKES

ALL OF THESE FESTIVE CAKES WERE augmented with foods from the market. We bought salted watermelon seeds and sweet lotus seeds, candied watermelon rind and lotus roots, and preserved dates to be set out for guests in a partitioned tray called *bat sin hop*, the "eight fairy basket," or "the tray of togetherness." We cut small stalks of sugarcane and peeled them down to their sweet cores. We picked, and bought, tangerines for good luck, oranges for sweetness and grapefruit and pomelos for abundance. A container of rice stood at the door with a scripted message attached: *Seong Moon,* meaning "Always Full," for visitors to see and thus share in our family's good fortune.

Small, potted fruit-bearing kumquat trees and flowering peach trees were brought home from the flower market, as were the freshly cut chrysanthemums so loved by my grandmother for their golden color, all to be displayed about her house. Her house, now cleaned, decorated, stocked with enough foods, cakes and snacks to please any number of guests who might drop in, was ready for New Year's Eve.

On this day before the great day, we always had a light breakfast of congee, then set up our New Year food displays. Out from storage came lacquered *guor hop,* or fruit baskets, to be polished until they gleamed, then crammed tight with standing sticks of sugarcane of varying lengths. Atop these we artfully arranged our sweet fruit, the oranges, tangerines, grapefruit and pomelos we had brought in earlier. Also out of storage came the partitioned tray that held our sweet snacks of melon seeds, nuts, sweet rinds and preserved dates.

From storage as well came three tall pewter ornaments, looking like bulbous vases, and called *fook look sau,* each standing for one of the great wishes of each New Year: good luck, long life and prosperity. A small table was brought out and put in front of the altar table in Ah Paw's living room, covered in a red, gold-embroidered cloth, to hold the tray of snacks and one of the pewter vases. The other vases went on the two sides of the altar, one for our family's ancestors, the other in front of Guan Gung, the god of protection.

Small fresh heads of lettuce, symbolizing prosperity, were bound together with scallions, for intelligence, and hung with red string from the doorjambs of my grandmother's living room and the two bedrooms of the house. This was the last preparation before going to the market to shop for the New Year's Eve banquet, the most important family meal of the Chinese year.

Throughout the day we cooked—the servants, my number-two aunt and myself—under Ah Paw's direction. Yet even before we ate, observances had to be made. As each dish was cooked, it had to be presented first as an offering at Ah Paw's altar, along with three cups of rice wine, three cups of tea, three bowls of rice and three pairs of chopsticks, so that our departed ancestors and the gods could dine with us. Drops of wine and tea would be drizzled on the floor in front of the altar for the gods to drink symbolically.

This offering of food completed, we would sit down to our annual Gau Dai Guai, the nine-course meal of New Year's Eve. Contrary to popular belief, a New Year's banquet is not a dinner of ten, twelve or more courses of exotic foods. Only nine courses were served; nine symbolizes never-ending infinity, and the foods served usually had to be *gau dai guai*, or "nine big dishes," reminders of wishes for the New Year. Often, my mother and brother would come to Ah Paw's house for this dinner, which made it happier for me. We would pull the table up to Ah Paw's divan, set all of the other chairs around it and have our New Year's Eve family meal.

Shrimp Balls

(Har Yuen)

The round shape of shrimp balls indicate togetherness, that there is no ending. They can be made of fish as well, but that they are made from shrimp, *har*, which sounds like laughter, suggests a dish of happiness. It is similar to the shrimp filling used as a stuffing in earlier recipes, but is only of shrimp, and special to the New Year.

¾ pound shrimp, shelled, deveined, washed, dried and chopped into a paste

3 tablespoons coriander, minced

2 tablespoons egg white, beaten

1 teaspoon sugar

½ teaspoon salt

Pinch white pepper

1 teaspoon light soy sauce

2 teaspoons oyster sauce

1½ teaspoons sesame oil

1½ teaspoons peanut oil

2 teaspoons Chinese white rice wine, or gin

8 cups cold water

1½ teaspoons salt

Place shrimp in a bowl, add all other ingredients except cold water and 1½ teaspoons salt and mix well to combine. I prefer mixing by hand. After it is well blended, pick up the shrimp mix and throw it with some force against a side of the bowl. Repeat about 10 times until mixture is firm. (If an electric mixer is used, mix 4 to 5 minutes, using flat paddle, until mixture is firm.)

Keep a small bowl of water close by to moisten hands. Divide mixture into 24 equal portions. Wet hands and roll each portion into a ball. The wetness will prevent sticking. Continue until 24 balls are made. Add cold water and 1½ teaspoons salt to a pot, bring to a boil over high heat. Add shrimp balls and return to a boil. Cook 3 to 4 minutes until shrimp balls are firm. Turn off heat, run cold water into pot to stop cooking and drain. Serve immediately.

MAKES 24 SHRIMP BALLS

Taro Root Pancakes

(LAI WU BOK BANG)

I truly enjoy making these taro root pancakes today as much as I did when I was a little girl. They were, and are, fun to make, and I make them from scratch. Usually I made them for Ah Paw to enjoy with her afternoon tea, but because Chinese bacon was available only in the cooler months around the New Year, she ordered it added to her pancakes. It thus became a New Year tradition for us, one I continue.

1½ pounds taro root, peeled, ends removed, coarsely grated (to yield 4 cups, tightly packed)

⅔ cup Chinese bacon, cut into ¼-inch dice

2 extra-large eggs

1 cup scallions, finely sliced

1½ teaspoons salt

2 teaspoons sugar

1½ teaspoons sesame oil

1 tablespoon Shao-Hsing wine, or sherry

Pinch white pepper

3 tablespoons cornstarch

7 tablespoons peanut oil

In a large bowl mix all ingredients except peanut oil, thoroughly to make a cohesive mass.

Heat a cast-iron skillet over high heat for 1 minute. Add 3 tablespoons peanut oil. When a wisp of white smoke appears, scoop 5 generous spoonfuls of taro root mixture (about 3 tablespoons each) into the pan and flatten them. Lower heat to medium-high and fry for 2 minutes. Turn over, fry for another 2 minutes until both sides are browned and crisp. Remove, drain on paper towels. Continue until all pancakes are done. With each batch you may have to add about 2 tablespoons peanut oil to the pan. When done, turn off heat, transfer to heated dish and serve.

MAKES 16 PANCAKES

White Cut Chicken

(Bok Chik Gai)

白
切
鷄

Chicken is a recurring food of the New Year. Its symbol is the phoenix, the bird that rose from its own ashes, and it symbolizes rebirth. That is one reason that I have given my granddaughter her Chinese name of Siu Fung, or Little Phoenix. This dish is a New Year must, but is a dish of choice at other feasts as well. It is called "white" because of its color after poaching. For offerings to our ancestors, it was always cooked with head and feet on, and presented whole, then cut up later to eat.

My grandmother insisted this dish be made with a fresh-killed chicken. Fresh-killed poultry is not so common these days, but if available it should be used, for it is best made with a chicken that has not been refrigerated.

> 10 cups cold water
>
> 3 scallions, trimmed, cut in half across
>
> 1 tablespoon salt
>
> 2 tablespoons sugar
>
> 1 4-pound chicken, fat and membranes removed, washed, cleaned thoroughly and drained

In a large pot or Dutch oven, place water, scallions, salt and sugar and bring to a boil over high heat. Place chicken in pot, breast side up, cover and return water to a boil. Lower heat, simmer 20 minutes. Turn chicken over in pot, cover pot again and simmer for another 20 minutes. Turn off heat. Allow chicken to rest in pot, covered, for another 30 minutes. Remove from pot, drain well, make certain there is no water in body cavity. Place on a chopping board and cut into bite-size pieces.

White Cut Chicken is best served room temperature with this dipping sauce of ginger and soy sauce.

Dipping Sauce

> 3 tablespoons light soy sauce
>
> 3 tablespoons Chicken Stock (page 13)

2 tablespoons minced ginger

4 tablespoons scallions, white portions only, finely sliced

1 teaspoon sesame oil

½ teaspoon sugar

Mix dipping sauce ingredients well, divide among small soy sauce dishes. Serve with the chicken.

SERVES 8

Salted Pork with Silken Bean Curd

(Ham Yuk Jiu Noon Dau Fu)

Pork always signifies prosperity at the New Year, and is represented, often more than once, in any observant banquet. This preparation also contains scallions or spring onions, a constant reminder of intelligence, its open stalk indicating an open mind. My grandmother loved this very soft, custardlike bean curd, which has a pleasant texture. These days it is often sold as "soft" or "silky" bean curd. She enjoyed it most with a spicy sauce that, she said, helped protect the body from dampness.

SAUCE

2 tablespoons hot bean sauce

1½ tablespoons Chinkiang vinegar

1 tablespoon oyster sauce

1½ tablespoons Shao-Hsing wine, or sherry

¼ teaspoon salt

2 teaspoons light soy sauce

1 teaspoon sesame oil

Pinch white pepper

½ cup Chicken Stock (page 13)

1½ tablespoons cornstarch

2 tablespoons peanut oil

2 teaspoons minced ginger

1 teaspoon minced garlic

½ cup onions, cut into ¼-inch dice

¼ cup scallions, white portions only, cut into ¼-inch pieces

½ cup Salted Pork (page 18), cut into ⅛-inch dice

1 19-oz. container soft bean curd, cut into ⅓-inch cubes

½ cup scallions, green portions only, finely sliced

Mix all ingredients for sauce; reserve.

Heat wok over high heat 30 seconds. Add peanut oil and coat wok with spatula. When a wisp of white smoke appears, add ginger and garlic, stir and cook 10 seconds. Add onions and white portions of scallions, mix and cook 3 minutes, until onions soften. Add pork, stir, cook for 2 minutes more. Make well in the mix, stir sauce, pour in, stir to mix, bring to a boil. Add bean curd, mix and return to a boil. Turn off heat immediately. Sprinkle with sliced green portions of scallions, mix well. Transfer to a heating dish and serve with cooked rice.

SERVES 4

Lotus Root Soup

(Lin Ngau Tong)

This was, and is, a Lunar New Year family heirloom. Its name is a play on words. The words for "lotus root" are *lin ngau*, which are almost identical to *lin yau*, which means "achieve more." Thus this soup is a New Year's greeting. It is also believed that the holes in the lotus root indicate that one should think things through. Lotus root comes in joined sections, quite like a sausage.

1½ pounds lotus root, each section separate, but left whole, washed thoroughly

8 cups cold water

1 slice ginger, 1 inch thick, lightly smashed

1½ pounds fresh pork butt, left whole

1 to 1½ teaspoons salt

2 scallions, finely sliced

In a large pot place lotus root, water and ginger, bring to a boil over high heat. Reduce heat, cover pot leaving a slight opening at the edge and allow to cook slowly for 30 minutes. Return to a boil, add pork, allow to return to a boil, lower heat, allow to simmer for 1 hour. At this point the lotus root should be tender. Test by inserting the end of a chopstick into the root. If it is cooked, the chopstick will enter easily. Add 1 teaspoon salt, stir, taste. Add additional salt if needed.

Remove lotus root and pork from soup. Cut root in half lengthwise, then slice it. Slice pork as well, and arrange both on a platter. Serve the dish as two courses together—the soup, hot, in bowls garnished with sliced scallions, the lotus root and pork with the following sauce.

Sauce

4 tablespoons Chicken Stock (page 13)

4 tablespoons light soy sauce

3 tablespoons finely sliced scallions

1 tablespoon sesame oil

1 teaspoon sugar

Mix all ingredients together, divide into individual soy sauce dishes and serve with lotus root and pork.

SERVES 6

Buddha's Delight

(Fat Choy Jai)

This classic dish was always served at Ah Paw's New Year's Eve dinner, as it was at my mother's, as it is at mine. It is at once a satisfying dish and an offering, a celebration of Buddhist vegetarianism. Its name alone, *fat choy*, wishes you prosperity for the year.

½ cup carrots, thinly sliced

⅓ cup bamboo shoots, thinly sliced

¾ cup lotus root, thinly sliced

3 water chestnuts, peeled, washed, thinly sliced

6 dried black mushrooms, soaked in water 30 minutes until softened, washed, stems removed and cut into julienne

30 pieces dried tiger lily buds, soaked, bottoms removed

¼ cup celery, cut into 1½-inch julienne

½ cup gingko nuts (page 250)

SAUCE

¼ teaspoon salt

1½ teaspoons sugar

1 tablespoon oyster sauce

1 teaspoon sesame oil

1½ teaspoons dark soy sauce

3 teaspoons cornstarch

Pinch white pepper

½ cup Vegetable Stock (page 14)

2½ to 3 tablespoons peanut oil

1 slice ginger, 1 inch thick, peeled

¾ teaspoon salt

1 tablespoon Shao-Hsing wine, or sherry

¼ cup Vegetable Stock

1 package (2 ounces) bean thread noodles, soaked 20 minutes until softened, drain, cut into 3-inch lengths

Arrange vegetables on a platter; reserve.

Combine all ingredients for sauce; set aside.

Heat wok over high heat for 45 seconds, add peanut oil, ginger and ¾ teaspoon salt. Coat wok with spatula. When a wisp of white smoke appears, begin adding vegetables. Stir-fry carrots and bamboo shoots, add lotus root, stir-fry 1 minute. Add all remaining vegetables, stir-fry 1 minute more. Drizzle wine into wok along its edges, mix well. Add vegetable stock, allow to cook 3 minutes until vegetables soften slightly.

Add bean thread noodles, stir together to mix. Make a well in the mixture, stir sauce, pour in, mix and cook for 1 minute. When sauce changes color to dark brown, turn off heat, transfer to a heated dish and serve.

SERVES 6

Steamed Fish

(Jing Yue)

In my grandmother's kitchen, and in mine, no dish was, or is, more important to the New Year celebration than a steamed fish. The word for fish is yue, which also translates as "plentiful." Also, the swimming motion of the fish connotes the concept of never-ending, or eternity. My grandmother always steamed a grass carp in a huge iron wok. In my kitchen I use a striped bass because it can be obtained in a size small enough to be steamed whole in a wok. It is important for the sake of tradition that the fish be steamed whole.

Steaming preserves the fish's flesh, its flavor and its shape. Variations of the traditional steamed fish often include shredded mushrooms, shredded pork, black beans or ginger and scallions. The recipe below is the original.

MARINADE

2 tablespoons light soy sauce

2 tablespoons Shao-Hsing wine, or sherry

2 tablespoons Scallion Oil (page 16)

4 tablespoons finely shredded ginger

1½ teaspoons sesame oil

1½ teaspoons Chinese white rice vinegar, or distilled white vinegar

¼ teaspoon salt

⅛ teaspoon white pepper

1 1½-pound fresh whole striped bass, scales, gills and intestines removed by fishmonger

7 cups boiling water

1 tablespoon Scallion Oil

2 scallions, finely sliced

1 tablespoon coriander, finely sliced

Mix ingredients for marinade well; reserve.

A FISH STEAMED IN MY HOME IN THE UNITED STATES,
EXACTLY AS I LEARNED TO DO IT FROM AH PAW.

Make certain fish is cleaned and washed well, inside and out. Make 3 cuts with a sharp knife in the side of the fish to the bone. Do not cut through. Repeat on other side. Dry fish well with paper towels and place in a steamproof dish. Pour marinade over fish and rub in with your hands, making certain to rub well into the cuts. Allow to rest 10 to 15 minutes.

Place a rack in a wok, add boiling water, place steamproof dish with fish on rack in wok and cover. Steam for about 10 to 15 minutes, or until the flesh seen in the cuts turns white and is firm. (See steaming directions, page 30.) Turn off heat. Pour scallion oil over fish, sprinkle with scallions and coriander and serve immediately.

SERVES 4, OR 6 AT A BANQUET

Fried Rice Yangzhou Style

(Yangzhou Chau Fan)

Always a component of any banquet of consequence, this is one of those dishes that transcends its region and becomes a universal favorite. Yangzhou is in Kiangsu Province, north of Shanghai, and when a special fried rice is desired for a banquet, invariably the version from Yangzhou is served. Ah Paw was no exception. It was her favorite festive rice and was always the penultimate dish of her New Year's Eve dinner. That it had, among its ingredients, the happiness of shrimp and the prosperity of pork only added to its attraction.

MARINADE

1 teaspoon light soy sauce

¼ teaspoon salt

½ teaspoon sugar

1½ teaspoons oyster sauce

1 teaspoon sesame oil

1 teaspoon Chinese white rice wine or gin mixed with ½ teaspoon ginger juice

Pinch white pepper

6 ounces shrimp, shelled and deveined, washed, dried and cut into ½-inch pieces

6½ tablespoons peanut oil

4 jumbo eggs, beaten with a pinch of white pepper and ¼ teaspoon salt

1½ cups diced Barbecued Pork (page 43), cut into ⅓-inch dice

2 teaspoons minced garlic

2 teaspoons minced ginger

5 cups Perfect Cooked Rice (page 11)

¾ tablespoon salt

2 tablespoons light soy sauce

4 scallions, finely sliced

Mix marinade in a bowl, add shrimp and allow to rest 15 minutes.

Stir-fry beaten eggs in 1½ tablespoons peanut oil until soft, but not dry, broken into small pieces, approximately 1 to 1½ minutes. Set aside. Wash wok and spatula and dry.

Stir-fry barbecued pork with 1 teaspoon minced garlic in 1 tablespoon peanut oil, until hot, approximately 2 minutes. Set aside. Wash wok and spatula and dry.

Stir-fry marinated shrimp mixture with 1 teaspoon minced garlic and 2 teaspoons minced ginger, in 1 tablespoon peanut oil, until shrimps turn pink, approximately 2 minutes. Wash wok and spatula and dry.

Heat wok over high heat 45 seconds, add 3 tablespoons peanut oil and ¾ teaspoon salt, coat wok with spatula. When a wisp of white smoke appears, add cooked rice, toss until well mixed, 3 to 4 minutes, until very hot. Add pork, mix thoroughly. Add shrimp, mix thoroughly. Add soy sauce, stir in, then add scrambled eggs, mix well. Add scallions and mix to combine all ingredients very thoroughly. Turn off heat, transfer to a heated platter and serve immediately.

SERVES 6 TO 8

Pan-Fried Noodles with Shredded Pork

(Yuk See Chau Mein)

Any New Year's Eve banquet was always concluded with a dish of noodles, simple or elaborate. This was, and is, one of the latter, but as Ah Paw would say when she requested that it be made, it is worth the effort. And she was right. Noodles, a recurring symbol of long life, were never cut when making this dish, in the belief that if one cut a noodle, a life might be shortened. The noodles are wedded to pork, that ubiquitous reminder of prosperity, which Ah Paw said had to be *yuk see*, shredded pork. Making this dish properly depends upon preparation and organization, upon having all ingredients, cut, measured and poured. Once you have cooked it well, you will be quite proud of yourself, as I was in my grandmother's kitchen.

MARINADE

2 teaspoons oyster sauce

1 teaspoon light soy sauce

¼ teaspoon salt

¾ teaspoon sugar

2 teaspoons sesame oil

1½ teaspoons Shao-Hsing wine, or sherry

1 teaspoon cornstarch

Pinch white pepper

6 ounces lean pork loin, shredded

SAUCE

1 teaspoon light soy sauce

¼ teaspoon salt

1½ teaspoons sugar

1 teaspoon sesame oil

1 tablespoon oyster sauce

1½ tablespoons cornstarch

Pinch white pepper

1 cup Chicken Stock (page 13)

8 cups cold water

½ cup bean sprouts, washed, drained

8 ounces thin fresh egg noodles such as capellini

2 teaspoons salt

5½ tablespoons peanut oil

2 teaspoons minced ginger

¼ cup Steamed Black Mushrooms (page 32) cut into julienne

3 scallions, trimmed, green portions cut into 2-inch sections, white portions quartered lengthwise

2 teaspoons minced garlic

Combine all ingredients for marinade in a bowl, add pork, mix well and allow to rest 15 minutes.

Mix all ingredients for sauce; reserve.

In a large pot, bring 8 cups cold water to a boil over high heat. Place bean sprouts in a strainer, lower into water for 6 to 8 seconds, remove, run cold water through strainer and reserve. Return water to a boil, add noodles and salt, stir and return again to a boil. Cook 1 minute, or until al dente, stirring with chopsticks to prevent sticking. Turn off heat, run cold water into the pot, drain through a strainer. Repeat twice, and allow noodles to drain thoroughly, about 30 minutes. Loosen noodles with chopsticks.

Heat a cast-iron skillet over high heat for 40 seconds. Add 2 tablespoons peanut oil to cover bottom. When a wisp of white smoke appears, place noodles in an even layer in the pan, covering entire bottom. Cook for 1 minute, moving pan about the burner to ensure noodles brown evenly. Control heat to prevent burning.

Turn noodles over: Slide noodles onto a large plate. Place similar plate over them, turn over and slide back into skillet. Add 1 tablespoon peanut oil to fry pan. Cook other side for 1 minute, moving pan as before.

As noodles cook, heat a wok over high heat for 40 seconds. Add 1½ tablespoons peanut oil and coat wok with spatula. Add ginger and stir. When ginger browns, approximately 45 seconds, add mushrooms and scallions. Stir and cook for 1 minute, or until green portions of scallions turn bright green. Turn off heat, remove from wok and reserve.

Wipe wok and spatula clean. Heat over high heat 30 seconds. Add remaining 1 tablespoon peanut oil, coat wok. When a wisp of white smoke appears, add minced garlic and stir for 15 seconds. When garlic browns, add pork and its marinade, spread in a thin layer. Stir, cook for 30 seconds, turn pork, mix, cook for 2 minutes. Add all reserved vegetables and mix well for 1 minute. Make a well in the center of the mix, stir sauce and pour in. Stir-fry all ingredients together until well mixed. When sauce bubbles and thickens, turn off heat. Transfer noodles to a heated platter, pour contents of wok over them and serve immediately.

SERVES 6

WE WOULD CLEAN UP AFTER DINNER, sweeping and dusting then hiding our brooms and dustpans because to see them on New Year' Day was bad luck. All of the women—Ah Paw, my mother, my aunts and the servants—would then comb their hair, because they could not comb it on New Year's Day, as it was another harbinger of bad luck. It was then I learned the importance of those porcelain pillows, which permit one to rest on her neck and shoulder without disturbing buns and hairdos.

It was time to wait, impatiently, for darkness to come, so we could go out with our lighted paper lanterns. On this last night of the old year, all of the younger girls and boys in the neighborhood would meet in the small square with our paper lanterns, wade though the sparkling firecrackers and lion dancers, and walk through Sah Gau "selling laziness." We would chant, in a singsong, *"Mai lan, mai lan, mai lan."*

Mai doh lin, sam sup man or, "Laziness for sale, laziness for sale, laziness for sale. Sell for a whole year," which meant that we were promising to get rid of any laziness we might display for the coming year. There was great fun doing this, much laughing and teasing of others, before returning to Ah Paw's house, there to wait until a call at the front door would notify us that the Fortune God had arrived.

This was a tradition reserved only for boys, young and just into their teens. They would write the characters for the Fortune God, Choi Sun, on strips of red paper, then go from door to door announcing that the Fortune God had arrived. Each family would give this representative of the god a red envelope of lucky money, called *lai see.* I was about nine or ten, I recall, and I asked Ah Paw why I could not carry the Fortune God's name from door to door. She told me that this was not for girls, but *bei lam jai jo*, only for boys.

When I asked why, she said she had just told me why and wouldn't I rather she tell me a story. Which meant I would get into her big bed with her and she would tell me the tale of *Guo Nin,* the legend of the New Year.

Five thousand years ago, she said, a wise emperor, through his astrologers, determined the planting seasons to help farmers. But it came to pass that after the sun had shown itself 365 times, a fearsome beast known as Nin would come to attack farmers and destroy their crops. But the farmers discovered that the beast feared noise, lights and the color red, so they kept their homes lighted, displayed papers and objects painted red, and set off firecrackers. This, Ah Paw said, was the beginning of the New Year celebration, and the phrase *Guo Nin* came to mean to "Go Past the Nin," defining the Lunar New Year.

It was why we had firecrackers, Ah Paw said, why we had the long sinuous lion dancers—both to remind us that we continue to keep Nin away. It was a familiar story to put me to sleep.

The next morning it was New Year's Day, and all of us in Ah Paw's house would greet each other with calls of *"Kung Hei Fat Choy,"* the traditional New Year greeting, which translates literally as "Congratulations, Good Fortune." For me this was a good meaning because as the youngest member of the household, I would be given *lai see* (lucky money) by everyone older than me, a custom I dearly loved. But first there was, on New Year's morning, a time to pay respects to the elders. That morning I wore all of the new clothes, my new dress, my new socks and shoes, before going into Ah Paw's living room.

Ah Paw would be seated in a big, blackwood chair in the center of her living room, with her altar behind her. My two aunts would come in, and each would bow to her, kneel and offer her a cup of tea. My grandmother would accept the cups, pour a bit from each cup on the floor in front of the altar, thus giving her ancestors and Guan Gung, the God of Protection, a drink. Ah Paw would then give each of my aunts a red, gold-embossed envelope of *lai see*, which contained money and a piece of evergreen branch, to denote life, as well as a tangerine, with stem and leaves, for sweetness.

My mother, Miu Hau, was next. She repeated the procedure of my aunts. She was followed by my brother, Ching Moh, and then my cousin. Ah Paw's two servants, Ah Guk and Sau Lin, were next. I was last to kneel, to serve tea and to receive my *lai see* from Ah Paw. But then the fun began. All of those older and married had to give me envelopes of lucky money as well.

These observances generally took up most of the morning, and then we ate our New Year's Day meal. This, too, was typically a family meal, but modest and not as elaborate as the New Year's Eve feast. It was also totally vegetarian. Ah Paw, as a practicing Buddhist, would eat no meat or fish on the New Year, and for the remaining two weeks that took the lunar observance to mid-month. Out of respect for her, we would prepare foods that we knew would please her, and eat as she ate.

Spring Rolls

(Chun Geun)

For the New Year, the spring roll represented a gold bar. It is made in various parts of China, with different fillings. This version was my grandmother's favorite, filled with vegetables and deemed by her to be a perfect temple offering before being eaten at home.

5 cups cold water

1 teaspoon salt

½ teaspoon baking soda (optional)

12 ounces (4½ cups, tightly packed) cabbage, washed, dried, cut into ¼-inch pieces across

PASTE

1½ tablespoons cornstarch, mixed with 1½ tablespoons cold water

½ cup boiling water

SAUCE

2 tablespoons oyster sauce

1 teaspoon light soy sauce

1 teaspoon sugar

1 teaspoon sesame oil

½ tablespoon Shao-Hsing wine, or sherry

2 tablespoons cornstarch

Pinch white pepper

½ cup cold water

2 tablespoons peanut oil

1 tablespoon minced ginger

3 scallions, trimmed, cut into 2-inch sections, white portions quartered lengthwise

7 Steamed Black Mushrooms (page 32), thinly sliced

16 spring roll skins

5 cups peanut oil (for deep-frying)

In a large pot place 5 cups water, salt and baking soda and bring to a boil over high heat. Add cabbage, submerge, stir and allow to cook for 40 seconds. Turn off heat, run cold water into pot, drain. Repeat, allow to drain 20 minutes and loosen cabbage with chopsticks. Reserve.

MAKE A PASTE: Place cornstarch-water mixture in a bowl. Stir with one hand, while gradually adding boiling water gradually with the other, until a smooth paste is created. Reserve.

Mix all ingredients for sauce in a small bowl; reserve.

Heat wok over high heat 40 seconds. Add 2 tablespoons peanut oil, coat wok with spatula. When a wisp of white smoke appears, add minced ginger and stir briefly. Add scallions, stir, cook 40 seconds. Add mushrooms and cabbage, mix well, cook for 3 minutes. Make a well in the mixture, stir sauce, pour in, stir well. When sauce thickens and bubbles, approximately 2 minutes, turn off heat. Transfer to a shallow dish, allow to come to room temperature. Refrigerate, covered, overnight.

MAKE SPRING ROLLS: Place 2 tablespoons filling in a line across one end of spring roll skin. Brush edges of skin with paste mixture. (Paste mixture should be prepared just prior to making spring rolls.) Fold over tip, continue to roll, folding in sides as you do. Keep brushing edges of skin with paste to ensure sealing. Repeat until all spring rolls are made.

Deep-fry spring rolls in 5 cups peanut oil at 350 degrees F, in 4 batches, until golden brown, 3 to 4 minutes for each batch. Keep turning to ensure even color. Remove from oil with tongs, drain through a strainer over a bowl, then remove to paper towels. Serve immediately.

MAKES 16 SPRING ROLLS

NOTE Spring rolls may be frozen after cooking. To reheat, either deep-fry lightly at 350 degrees F for 2 minutes, or until crisp; or place in a 375-degree F oven for 3 minutes on each side, until hot and crisp.

Fried Oysters

(JAH SANG HO)

Oysters are one of those three fruits of the sea permissible to Buddhists and were therefore insisted upon for New Year lunch by my grandmother. Cooking them with a batter is traditional. Their name, *ho see*, sounds like the Chinese words for good business.

BATTER

1½ cups bleached all-purpose, high-gluten flour

10 ounces cold water

¾ teaspoon salt

2 tablespoons baking powder

2 tablespoons peanut oil

5 cups peanut oil

20 medium-size fresh oysters, opened, removed from shells, patted dry, dusted with flour

Combine all batter ingredients in a bowl and reserve.

Heat wok over high heat for 1 minute. Pour in peanut oil, heat to 375 degrees F. Dip each oyster into the batter until well coated. When a wisp of white smoke appears, lower oysters into oil. Deep-fry 5 at a time until light brown, about 3 minutes. Remove oysters, place in strainer, drain over a bowl.

Deep-fry last batch to a golden brown, about 4 minutes. Place cooked oysters back in oil for 2 minutes more so they become golden brown. During frying, always control heat. You may need to lower if oysters brown too much, or raise if they cook too slowly.

SERVES 4 TO 6

Spinach Stir-Fried with Garlic

(SEUN YUNG CHAU BOR CHOI)

蒜蓉炒菠菜

The name for spinach in Chinese is *bor choi*, or "the vegetable that waves," an accurate description of its leaves. Like other leafy vegetables, it is a felicitous New Year reminder of paper money. Because of its direct taste, it is best enjoyed simply, in this case, complemented with garlic. Ah Paw liked to add that the deep green the spinach acquired after blanching also reminded her of jade.

8 cups cold water

1½ teaspoons salt

1 slice ginger, 1½ inch thick, lightly smashed

¾ teaspoon baking soda (optional)

1 pound fresh spinach, washed well 3 times to remove grit, drained and individual stalks separated, each cut in half, across

2½ tablespoons peanut oil

1½ tablespoons minced garlic

In a pot place water, 1 teaspoon salt, ginger and baking soda and bring to a boil over high heat. Add spinach, submerge completely, water-blanch for 30 seconds. Turn off heat, run cold water into pot. Drain spinach well. Reserve.

Heat wok over high heat 30 seconds. Add peanut oil and remaining ½ teaspoon salt and coat wok with spatula. When a wisp of white smoke appears, add garlic, stir 30 seconds, or until garlic turns light brown. Add spinach, stir-fry together 2 to 3 minutes, until very hot. Keep spinach sections as separate as possible so they will be well coated with minced garlic. Turn off heat, transfer to a heated dish and serve immediately.

SERVES 4 TO 6

Lima Bean Soup with Sour Mustard Pickle

(CHON DAU SEUN CHOI TONG)

For our New Year visitors, my grandmother's servants prepared lima beans in a special way. They allowed them to harden, then deep-fried them and sprinkled them with salt, to be eaten as a snack. But they were also cooked fresh, alone or in combination with other vegetables, in this instance in a soup, made pleasantly tart with the addition of sour mustard pickle.

4½ cups Vegetable Stock (page 14)

1 slice ginger, 1 inch thick, lightly smashed

1 cup sour mustard pickle, cut into ¼-inch dice

1½ cups fresh lima beans (if frozen, allow to come to room temperature)

1 teaspoon sugar

4 teaspoons light soy sauce

4 tablespoons Scallion Oil (page 16)

2 small cakes fresh bean curd, cut into ½-inch cubes

3 tablespoons coriander, finely sliced

In a large pot, place vegetable stock, ginger and mustard pickle, cover and bring to a boil over high heat. Lower heat to medium, allow to simmer 7 minutes. Add lima beans, cook for 5 minutes more. Add sugar, soy sauce and scallion oil, stir well. Return to a boil, add bean curd, allow to come to a boil and cook 2 minutes more. Turn off heat, stir in coriander. Remove soup to a heated tureen and serve.

SERVES 4 TO 6

Mussels with Ginger and Scallions

(Geung Chung Chau Hak Hin)

Our name for mussels, *hak hin*, translates as "black clams." It is another of those shellfish permitted to be eaten by vegetarian Buddhists, and Ah Paw loved them.

SAUCE

2½ tablespoons oyster sauce

1½ teaspoons dark soy sauce

1¼ teaspoons sugar

1 teaspoon Chinese white rice vinegar, or distilled white vinegar

2 teaspoons sesame oil

1 tablespoon Shao-Hsing wine, or sherry

4 teaspoons cornstarch

Pinch white pepper

1 cup Vegetable Stock (page 14)

10 cups water

2 pounds mussels, sand and beards removed, washed thoroughly until clean

2½ tablespoons peanut oil

3 tablespoons shredded ginger

1 cup scallions, trimmed, cut into 1-inch pieces

Mix all ingredients for sauce; reserve.

In large pot, place water, cover, bring to a boil over high heat. Add mussels, stir. When mussels open, remove with a slotted spoon and place in a large bowl. Reserve. Discard any mussels that do not open.

Heat wok over high heat for 45 seconds, add peanut oil, coat wok with spatula. When a wisp of white smoke appears, add ginger and stir 30 seconds. Turn off heat. Stir sauce, pour into wok. Turn heat back to high and stir sauce. Add mussels, mix until they are thoroughly coated, about 2 to 3 minutes, and sauce thickens. Add scallions and mix all ingredients well. Turn off heat and transfer to a heated dish, serve immediately.

SERVES 4 TO 6

WITH THIS MEAL WE ATE BOWLS of cooked rice, and concluded it with sweet oranges, tangerines and pomelos. Then we awaited the parade of guests who visited Ah Paw this first day of the new lunar year. To receive her guests she did not sit in the big carved chair as she had with her family in the morning, but went to the comfort of her divan to welcome in the New Year with a whole host of neighbors, friends and acquaintances from Sah Gau.

Everyone who came through her door was welcome, and the servants and I were kept busy pouring cups of tea, slicing rice cakes, steaming or pan-frying turnip, taro root and water chestnut cakes and passing the tray of sweet and salted seeds and nuts, as well as the candied and preserved fruit.

Any unmarried children who came to her living room received a *lai see* envelope. Likewise, any visitors came with envelopes for me, my brother and my cousin. This pattern of receiving guests continued into the next day, the second day of the New Year, which was also a special day for Ah Paw, what she called her day of Hoi Lin, a day of prayer that truly opened the New Year.

She would pray continuously through the morning and afternoon, as firecrackers exploded unceasingly in the streets outside, and while we prepared yet another banquet. This was also an important family meal, and although it included many, if not most of the other festive and symbolic dishes of the preceding days, it was most notable for a most significant preparation of an almost-live raw fish.

Fish Alive

(Yue Sahn)

This was a dish of great importance, made from a grass carp pulled fresh from one of Ah Paw's ponds, a dish which, although she could not eat in the New Year because of her vegetarian beliefs, she ordered prepared for her family. Most people these days associate raw fish dishes with the Japanese table, but in China this was a tradition of centuries in which the fish had to be killed just minutes before serving. Yue Sahn was reserved for this second day of the New Year, as part of a family dinner before a wedding, a must for a sixtieth birthday celebration, traditionally a milestone in one's longevity, or for any family gathering of great import.

The fish would be brought to my grandmother's kitchen by Ah Guk and Sau Lin, her "Chrysanthemum" and "Beautiful Lotus" servants. It was my job to stun it with a blow to its head, remove its scales, slit its body, cleanse its insides and remove its gills. Ah Guk and Sau Lin would carefully slice it and serve it at once.

Because Ah Paw believed this raw fish was only for adults and too strong to be digested by a small child such as myself, I was not permitted to eat it. I could help prepare it, but I was forbidden to eat it. In fact, it was not until I was sixteen years old and living in Hong Kong that I actually ate Yeu Sahn. Instead I, and other youngsters in the family, would be given bowls of chicken congee.

1 5-pound grass carp, whole, live

Have the fishmonger prepare fish in this manner: Remove scales, gills and intestines. Cut fish open along its length, butterflying it whole. Have backbone removed, so that there are two halves without a backbone. Cut along the back of the fish where bone had been. Do not use section that contains stomach. Remove skin from two lengths, then slice fish crosswise into slices ⅛-inch thick.

Layer slices in a platter, serve with the following dipping sauce.

Dipping Sauce

4½ tablespoons Chicken Stock (page 13)

2 tablespoons dark soy sauce

2 tablespoons light soy sauce

1 tablespoon Chinese red rice vinegar, or red wine vinegar

2 small red hot chiles, minced

1½ tablespoons Chinese white rice wine, or gin

2 tablespoons scallions, finely sliced

1 tablespoon minced ginger

1 tablespoon Scallion Oil (page 16)

⅛ teaspoon white pepper

Combine all ingredients for dipping sauce. Divide dip into small soy sauce dishes and serve with fish slices.

THIS FISH WOULD SERVE AS MANY AS 20 PEOPLE IN AH PAW'S HOUSE; A SMALLER FISH MAY BE USED

VISITORS CONTINUED TO COME THROUGH THE next day, and the next, up to seven days, when it was expected that relatives and family from far distances would make their way to Ah Paw's house. On that seventh day of the New Year it was *Yan Yat*, or "Everybody's Birthday," a day for some families to visit temples with food offerings for the gods, then to return home for still another festive meal.

This was not the case with Ah Paw. I remember her telling me that we as a family had eaten a sufficient number of meals in this early part of the New Year and it was time to rest until the Lantern Festival.

SIX

THE LANTERN FESTIVAL:
DINING WITH THE NUNS

THE LANTERN FESTIVAL, WHICH ALWAYS FALLS on the fifteenth day after the Lunar New Year, marks the official end of the annual New Year observance. It is a colorful conclusion, with displays of brightly dyed, inventive and often quite elaborate paper lanterns that are lighted to honor Sheung Yeun, Lord of all the Heavenly Gods, on his birthday. This festival of light, not only of lanterns, but of countless lighted candles, is commonly known as *Yeun Siu*, a shortened version of Sheung Yeun's name.

Observed by Buddhists and Taoists alike, it was for me a day of wonder, of processions and fireworks, of lanterns shaped like animals, temples, houses and boats, often decorated painstakingly with calligraphy honoring Sheung Yeun. And it was a time to eat small, round boiled glutinous rice dumplings, *tong yeun*, filled with sweet

sesame paste, crushed peanuts or lotus seed paste, served six at a time in bowls of the sugary liquid in which they had been boiled.

At Ah Paw's house we made these by the dozen, eating them ourselves and offering their sweetness and roundness to others as gestures of friendship and unity. We would take our bowls of *tong yeun* out into the street and eat them as we watched the lanterns drift by.

But my grandmother, as she always did, had a celebration of the Lantern Festival like no other. It had begun, she told me, during the years of the Chinese-Japanese War, just about the time when I was born. At a far boundary of Sah Gau stood a temple, within the walled compound of which lived a group of Buddhist nuns.

It had been a difficult time for women in southern China, Ah Paw would tell me. In Sah Gau alone, she told me, there were too many women who were *sik loon fan*, who "ate soft rice"—that is food they didn't earn, but who had been supported by husbands who had gone to the United States to earn money and who sent them periodical support. The Japanese occupation of much of eastern and southern China stopped this flow of money, and many of these women were forced to sell plots of land, pieces of furniture and parts of their houses.

The *see gu*, these nuns, Ah Paw said, despite not having much more than the taros and sweet potatoes they grew, would come to Sah Gau and pray for these women, which my grandmother believed was a noble thing to do. Often people would give the nuns some vegetables, a couple of pieces of fruit, whatever could be spared. Also, in that time of war shortages the nuns had no peanut oil with which to cook, because it was most scarce. "Ah Fei," my grandmother told me. "It was not too hard for us, for we could render the fat from a pig and have cooking oil, but the nuns could eat nothing from animals." So Ah Paw took it upon herself to collect peanut oil for the nuns, and people throughout the town would bring ounces, spoonfuls, whatever they could spare and dribble it into bottles, which were then given to the nuns.

Over the years my grandmother's adoption of the nuns grew into an annual tradition in which the order of nuns would be invited to Ah Paw's house on the day of the Lantern Festival, for a vegetarian feast of friendship to close out the New Year observance. And on this fifteenth day of the New Year, after we had eaten our *tong yeun*, after we had watched processions of lanterns, we awaited our guests, the four nuns, to arrive from their temple grounds.

The *see gu* would come slowly up the street to Ah Paw's house, their shaven heads gleaming, their drab gray cotton robes down to their ankles touching gray felt sandals, chanting prayers to the health of Sah Gau as they walked, one rhythmically tapping a round, hollow wood gourd with a stick, another hitting a small gong, the others clacking tiny cymbals until they arrived. We would welcome them into the house and to Ah Paw's altar, where they would offer prayers to her ancestors, prayers for the continued health of our family and for a plentiful New Year.

I remember them as quite shy, and they had to be coaxed to the table in Ah Paw's living room set for them and for us, to eat the meal that she had arranged for us to cook for them, a meal she dubbed *See Gu Yin Jik*, "The Banquet of the Nuns," or equally, *Bat Dai Guai*, "Eight Precious Dishes," because of the lucky connotation of the number eight in China, where it is synonymous with prosperity.

"M'ho gum hak jik," Ah Paw repeated several times over, waving the women to chairs. "Don't be bashful."

Then, when they were finally seated, Ah Paw told them, *"Mo sung, Du ill sek bau fon,"* a humble, modest recitation of manners, which translates as "If there is not enough food for you, we have plenty of rice to fill your stomachs." It was not, of course, meant to be taken literally because there was more than sufficient food set out, but simply good manners, a confession of humility. And then we ate, the nuns and us.

Vegetarian Eggs

(Jai Gai Dan)

This is a most popular preparation among religious Buddhists. When cooked, these imitations look like eggs that have been cooked in soy sauce.

2 large (1¼ pounds total) baking potatoes, unpeeled

6 cups cold water

½ cup wheat starch

7 ounces water

1¾ teaspoons sugar

1 teaspoon salt

1 teaspoon five-spice powder

3 tablespoons peanut oil

1 cup cornstarch, for dusting

6 cups peanut oil, for deep-frying

In a pot place potatoes and 6 cups water, bring to a boil over high heat. Lower heat to medium-high and cook for 45 minutes. Turn off heat, drain and allow potatoes to cool. Peel, mash and reserve.

Place wheat starch in a bowl. Bring 7 ounces water to a boil and add to wheat starch. Mix quickly with wooden spoon to blend. Add mashed potatoes, sugar, salt, five-spice powder and 3 tablespoons peanut oil and mix into a smooth dough. Divide into 12 equal portions. Roll each into an egg shape and dust with cornstarch.

Heat wok over high heat, 40 seconds. Add 6 cups peanut oil. When a wisp of white smoke appears, place 3 of the "eggs" into a Chinese strainer, lower into oil. Fry 3 to 4 minutes, turning, until golden brown. Drain, reserve, in a warm oven. Repeat until all 12 are cooked. Serve immediately.

SERVES 4 TO 6

Clams Steamed with Ginger and Scallions

(Geung Chung Jing Hin)

Clams are the fruit of the sea that represent prosperity and are, to be sure, permissible to eat by observant Buddhists, including nuns.

SAUCE

2 teaspoons minced ginger

3 tablespoons scallions, finely sliced

1 tablespoon light soy sauce

1½ tablespoons Shao-Hsing wine, or sherry

1½ teaspoons sugar

1½ teaspoons Chinese white rice vinegar, or distilled white vinegar

1 tablespoon Scallion Oil (page 16)

3 tablespoons Vegetable Stock (page 14)

Pinch white pepper

12 clams, medium, opened on the half-shell by a fishmonger

8 cups boiling water

6 sprigs coriander

Combine sauce ingredients in a bowl. Place clams in a steamproof dish. Stir sauce, pour over clams. Place dish on a rack in a wok over 6 cups boiling water, cover and steam, 1½ to 2 minutes. Do not oversteam, or clams will become tough (see steaming directions, page 30). Turn off heat and remove dish from steamer. Garnish with coriander and serve immediately.

MAKES 12 CLAMS

Romaine Lettuce with Black Beans

(Dau See Chau Sahng Choi)

豆鼓炒生菜

The only lettuce I knew in China is a variety almost identical in appearance to romaine. In China, all lettuce is *sahng choi*. This particular lettuce, which grew in profusion in Ah Paw's walled garden, looks like romaine but has a paler color and a texture quite like iceberg lettuce. It is called *bor lei sahng choi*, or "glass lettuce."

7 cups cold water

1 teaspoon salt

¼ teaspoon baking soda, optional

1¼ pounds romaine lettuce, washed and drained, wilted leaves discarded, cut into 2-inch pieces, and stalks separated from leaves (yield will be about 1 pound)

SAUCE

2 teaspoons Shao-Hsing wine, or sherry

2 tablespoons oyster sauce

1 teaspoon sesame oil

2 teaspoons light soy sauce

1 teaspoon sugar

Pinch white pepper

2 teaspoons cornstarch

2 tablespoons Vegetable Stock (page 14)

2½ tablespoons peanut oil

¼ teaspoon salt

3 cloves garlic, peeled, lightly smashed

1½ tablespoons fermented black beans, washed twice and drained

In a large pot place water, add salt and baking soda if using, cover and bring to a boil over high heat. Add lettuce stalks, stir, 5 seconds. Add leaves, submerge completely, cook 5 seconds more. Turn off heat, run cold water into pot, drain well. Toss lettuce to ensure dryness, reserve.

Mix sauce ingredients, reserve.

Heat wok over high heat 30 seconds. Add peanut oil and salt and coat wok with spatula. When a wisp of white smoke appears, add garlic and black beans. Stir and mix well, 20 seconds, until garlic turns light brown. Add reserved lettuce, mix well, making sure the leaves and stalks are coated and very hot, about 1½ minutes. Make a well in the center of the mix, stir sauce, pour in and mix well. When sauce thickens and bubbles, turn off heat, transfer to a heated dish and serve with cooked rice.

SERVES 4 TO 6

Gingko Nuts Stir-Fried with Snow Peas

(Bok Guor Chau Seut Dao)

These little egg-shaped nuts of the gingko tree were always served during the New Year. They possess no particular symbolism, but they were, and are, a continuing tradition. In Sah Gau we would buy them fresh in the shell, then once in Ah Paw's kitchen it was always my job to break their shells with a mallet, discard the shells and prepare them. Once boiled, and peeled, their lovely yellow color adds to the beauty of any dish.

These days gingko nuts come canned, and they are quite fine if a little softer than those fresh. In the many Chinatowns, you may encounter sidewalk tables behind which small groups of elderly women sit, cracking gingko shells and shelling the nuts as they tell passersby how good the nuts are for their systems. Preparing fresh gingko nuts is time-consuming, so I usually recommend using the canned ones. But if you prefer the satisfaction of preparing your foods from scratch, then follow the instructions below.

> ½ cup gingko nuts, canned, or ¾ cup fresh, shelled, to yield ½ cup
>
> 2 tablespoons peanut oil
>
> 1 slice ginger, ½ inch thick, lightly smashed
>
> ½ teaspoon salt
>
> ½ cup scallions, white portions only, cut into ¼-inch pieces, on the diagonal
>
> 8 ounces snow peas, strings removed, washed and drained, and cut into thirds on the diagonal
>
> 2 tablespoons Vegetable Stock (page 14)

Drain and reserve canned gingko nuts, or prepare fresh: Crack gingko nut shells, discard. Place 3 cups of water in a pot, bring to a boil. Add nuts to boiling water, return to a boil, reduce heat and cook nuts for 10 minutes. Turn off heat, run cold water into pot, pour off. Skin the nuts, pull off small bitter stems, reserve. This will yield ½ cup nuts.

Heat wok over high heat for 45 seconds. Add peanut oil, coat wok with spatula. When a wisp of white smoke appears, add ginger and stir 30 seconds, until ginger releases its fragrance. Add salt, stir. Add scallions, stir, cook 20 seconds. Add snow peas, stir, cook 20 seconds. Add gingko nuts, stir to mix well, cook 4 minutes, or until snow peas become bright green. If mixture is too dry, you may need to add 1 to 2 tablespoons of stock. Turn off heat, transfer to a heated dish and serve.

SERVES 4 TO 6

Steamed Whole Wintermelon Soup

(Bat Boh Dong Gua Jung)

This grand and unusual dish was always the centerpiece of Ah Paw's feast for the Buddhist nuns. The wintermelon itself became both the cooking pot for the soup and the serving tureen, for the soup brewed in it. Its name, *bat boh*, means "eight treasures," and had a double meaning for Ah Paw: eight treasured ingredients in the soup, as part of a dinner of eight treasured dishes, a very lucky *Seung Bat*, or "Double Eight."

3 cups water

½ cup peanuts

1 10-pound wintermelon

¾ cup gingko nuts, canned, or 1 cup fresh, to yield ¾ cups (see page 160)

½ cup straw mushrooms, cut into quarters

½ cup dried black mushrooms. soak until softened, washed and stems discarded, caps cut into ⅓-inch dice

½ cup carrots, cut into ⅓-inch dice

½ cup bamboo shoots, cut into ⅓-inch dice

⅓ cup water chestnuts, peeled, washed, dried and cut into ⅓-inch dice

½ cup green peas, fresh or frozen

1 tablespoon minced ginger

1 teaspoon minced garlic

2 teaspoons salt

4 tablespoons Scallion Oil (page 16)

5½ cups Vegetable Stock (page 14)

In a small pot, bring 3 cups water to a boil. Add peanuts, lower heat, simmer 20 minutes. Turn off heat, drain and reserve.

For this you will need a very large pot, such as a clam pot with a steaming insert, or a large stock pot and a rack. Place wintermelon in large pot: Put a rack on bottom of pot, place melon on it. With a pencil, mark melon where it is even with the top of the pot. Remove melon and rack from pot. Cut melon straight across top at the measurement line. Discard top.

Using a small serrated grapefruit knife, remove pulp and seeds from melon. Create a serrated edge around the top of the melon. Place peanuts and all other ingredients, except vegetable stock, in the melon cavity. Set aside.

Tie the ends of 6 lengths of string to the rim of the rack. Place melon on the rack, bring strings up and over the melon and join together in one knot. The strings should be taut to secure the melon. Pour 2 to 3 inches of water into the pot and bring to a boil.

Lift the melon by the strings, lower into boiling water. Add vegetable stock. Cover pot and steam for at least 1 hour. After that hour, check every 8 to 10 minutes to see if melon is tender. A young melon should cook to tenderness in 1 hour, an older one will require more steaming. As melon steams, check pot to see if more boiling water is needed. Do not overcook or the outer skin of melon will begin to sag. The melon and the soup are done when the inside of the melon is tender.

Turn off heat. Lift melon and rack by the strings and place on a plate. Cut strings and remove. Ladle soup into individual bowls, carefully shaving pieces of melon interior and adding 1 or 2 shavings to each bowl.

SERVES AT LEAST 10

Steamed Eggplant

(Jing Ai Guah)

The eggplants in Ah Paw's garden—for that matter, throughout most of China—were, and are, different from the eggplants that most people are familiar with today. They are not big and bulbous, but rather thin and up to twelve inches long, and either glossy purple or white in color. These days such eggplants are referred to as "Chinese eggplants" and are available in Asian markets.

3–4 (1 pound total) Chinese eggplants, stems removed

2 tablespoons peanut oil

½ onion, cut into ⅛-inch dice

1 tablespoon sesame seed paste

¼ cup Vegetable Stock (page 14)

3 hot red chiles, minced

1 tablespoon Shao-Hsing wine, or sherry

1½ teaspoons sugar

¾ teaspoon salt

1 teaspoon Chinese white rice vinegar, or distilled white vinegar

1 tablespoon sesame oil

3 tablespoons scallions, green portions, finely sliced

Prepare eggplants: Place whole eggplants in a steamer. Steam for 6 minutes (see steaming directions, page 30), until a chopstick easily pierces the flesh. Turn off heat, remove from heat and place in a long dish. With a chopstick, "cut" along length of each eggplant to open in half. Then, with chopstick, draw along the lengths again to create strips. Reserve.

As eggplants steam, prepare the sauce; Heat wok over high heat for 30 seconds. Add peanut oil, coat wok with spatula. When a wisp of white smoke appears, add onions. Stir, lower heat to medium and cook 3 minutes, until soft. Add sesame seed paste, stock and chiles, mix well, until paste liquefies, and liquid boils. Add all other ingredients, except scallions, mix together thoroughly. When sauce boils, turn off heat. Pour sauce over eggplant strips, sprinkle with scallions and serve immediately.

SERVES 4 TO 6

Noodles with Young Ginger

(Ji Geung Lo Mein)

At the New Year, noodles represent longevity. Because of this they were never cut when preparing them, and to serve them was to wish those who ate them a long life. In Sah Gau there were many varieties and shapes of noodles, and for vegetarians there were noodles made without eggs. These are what were served to the nuns, along with that special food that came usually with the onset of the New Year, young ginger, more subtle, less hot than the customary kind. These days this young, often pinkish gingerroot is available year-round. This dish illustrates what a "lo mein" is—that is, a dish tossed together, not precisely stir-fried.

SAUCE

1½ tablespoons oyster sauce

2 teaspoons light soy sauce

1 teaspoon sugar

1 tablespoon Shao-Hsing wine, or sherry

4 tablespoons Vegetable Stock (page 14)

1 teaspoon sesame oil

Pinch white pepper

8 cups cold water

2 teaspoons salt

8 ounces fresh, flat eggless noodles, like linguine

3 tablespoons peanut oil

4 tablespoons young ginger, shredded (if unavailable regular ginger may be used)

1 cup scallions, cut into 2-inch pieces, white portions quartered lengthwise

Combine all ingredients for sauce; set aside.

In a large pot place water and salt and bring to a boil over high heat. Add noodles, cook 45 seconds to 1 minute, or al dente, stirring and loosening them with chopsticks as they cook. Turn off heat, run cold water into pot, drain noodles immediately through a strainer. Place noodles back into pot and fill with cold water. Mix with hands, drain again through strainer. Repeat until noodles are cool. Allow to drain 10 to 15 minutes, loosening with chopsticks. Reserve.

Heat wok over high heat 45 seconds. Add peanut oil, coat wok with spatula. When a wisp of white smoke appears, add ginger, stir-fry 45 seconds. Stir sauce, pour in, mix well, allow to boil. Add noodles, stir, mix so noodles absorb the sauce. Add scallions, stir together for 2 minutes. Turn off heat, transfer to a heated dish and serve immediately.

SERVES 4 TO 6

Red Bean Soup

(Hung Dau Sah)

This sweet soup has always been a traditional dish of the Lantern Festival, and as such, was a perfect ending to Ah Paw's dinner for her adopted nuns. It can be eaten hot or warm and, according to my grandmother, was extraordinarily healthy and increased one's blood supply. Chinese red beans are small, about the size of mung beans, and come in 1-pound packages. This recipe produces a soup that is moderately sweet. It can be made sweeter with the addition of more sugar, to taste.

½ pound Chinese red beans
6 cups cold water
5 ounces rock sugar or brown sugar

Place beans in a pot, cover with cold tap water and wash 2 times by rubbing between palms to remove grit. Drain. Place beans back in pot, add 6 cups cold water, cover and bring to a boil over high heat. Stir beans, lower heat, leave a small opening at the cover and allow to simmer 1 hour until beans are very tender. If beans are not tender, add ¼ cup boiling water. Stir occasionally to avoid sticking.

When beans are tender and breaking apart, add sugar. Cook, stirring until sugar dissolves, about 5 to 7 minutes for rock sugar, immediately for brown sugar. Turn off heat, pour into a heated tureen and serve immediately.

SERVES 4 TO 6

More Lessons from Ah Paw's Table

Very soon after the nuns had concluded their meal with fresh oranges and tangerines, they prepared to return to their temple compound. But first Ah Paw had to remind the nuns not to forget the envelopes of *lai see*, lucky money, she had given to them on their arrival. They in turn prayed again to Ah Paw's ancestors and to all of us, thanking us for their meal, and then they left, their chants and the tones of their gourds, gongs and cymbals turning to whispers the farther away they went. My aunt, the servants and I cleaned the dinner table, then they left for their respective beds and I was summoned by Ah Paw to her bed because, she said, the goodness she felt because of the nuns' presence had reminded her of some tales of behavior that she thought I should be made aware of. These stories were, as was Ah Paw's custom, personal parables, and as always, she used food to demonstrate her lessons.

A husband, Ah Paw related, went off to a faraway land to earn money for his family, leaving his wife and his mother at home. The wife, it seemed, was not pleasant to her mother-in-law, and would eat the best food, saving only scraps for the mother-in-law. Most often, these were small bits of cartilage, with very little fish meat attached, called *yu tau sah*, or "fish head sand," from the heads of the cooked fish.

The mother-in-law knew what was happening, said nothing, but kept saving these bits in a jar, which she showed to her son when he returned. The son, a wise man, disguised himself as a peddler and walked through the village announcing that he was a buyer of fish head sand. His mother, happy, jumped up with jar, which the disguised son bought for a great deal of money, money she promptly showed to her daughter-in-law. The daughter-in-law changed overnight, Ah Paw said. She began eating those small bits of fish and saving the pieces of cartilage until she had a huge jar of fish head sand, waiting for the peddler to return and buy them.

Of course, no peddler ever appeared again, and the mean daughter-in-law was left with her jar of *yu tau sah*. And what did this mean? Ah Paw asked me rhetorically. Then she answered that what the story demonstrated was first, that one should not be selfish, should never mistreat anyone and finally, should always see first to the care and comfort of the elderly.

Nor was this story the end to that evening. It seemed that there was another elderly woman, half-blind, who was tended to by a young female servant. The servant, after cooking, always took *fan sum*, the "heart of the rice," or best of the pot, for herself and gave that less good to her mistress. The woman complained to her son and said she wanted him to discharge the servant, but the son, also a wise man, said he would solve the problem.

That evening, as they were eating, the son, pretending to be talking only to his mother, but loud enough for the servant to overhear, mentioned that he had heard from a medical scholar that if a young person ate only the heart of the rice, he or she would develop heart failure. Never again, related Ah Paw, did the servant attempt to deceive the blind woman.

"And this, Ah Fei, means what?" my grandmother asked me. Share equally, I remember answering her, and Ah Paw nodded, but was there not something more? Never take advantage of anyone, ever. This pleased Ah Paw. But was there not something else I had perhaps forgotten when considering those of whom one should never take advantage? Perhaps the elderly, I said, a simultaneous response and question. To which my grandmother smiled with pleasure. I had at last understood the message.

SEVEN

FAMILY FEASTS AND
FOLKLORE FESTIVALS

CLEARLY, THE EXTENDED LUNAR NEW YEAR observance, which ended formally with the Lantern Festival, fifteen days into the new year, was the most important festival of our year. Yet just as important to my grandmother's family, and thus to mine, were other holidays rooted in religion, mythology, folklore and custom, some observed widely, others simply feasts particular to our family—dates and occasions important to us as a family, many of which involved honoring ancestors. Significant to all of these were the particular foods we ate to observe them.

Many familiar, favored dishes recurred at these festivals, celebrations and family gatherings throughout the year. White cut chicken was always brought to the temple, as well as to the graveyard as an ancestral offering. On the eves of weddings and birthdays the serving of just-killed raw fish, which we knew as Fish Alive, was a given, as were congees of fish and chicken, and traditional steamed fish.

When we were to welcome guests, Ah Paw always preached that we had to pick our best, and cook it with skill and respect for these guests. "Ah Fei, you must always offer your best," she would say. And more often than not, many of the dishes she would dictate as her choices would be those requiring some effort and time. It was important to her, and an aspect of food presentation she taught to me, that when cooking for guests, whether family or not, the dishes prepared and served should demonstrate respect for our guests and inspire some wonder, even awe. By their very appearance they should indicate that they took time and effort to prepare, thus honoring guests not only with the food, but the effort as well.

Guests would always arrive at Ah Paw's house expecting the best, she would say, and that is what must be given to them. It was an axiom of hers that only the choicest should be cooked for her visitors. *"Han gei, but han yan,"* she would teach. "Do not spend for yourself, spend for your guests." It was a most tangible way of "giving face," or *bei min*, that uniquely Chinese expression that is the equivalent of giving respect by demonstrating humility.

With all of these observant dates, family or otherwise, foods would be cooked, then symbolically shared with a god, or with an ancestor, before being cut up and served to family and guests. For example, white cut chicken, offered most often during any year, would be cooked whole, then brought to altar, temple or grave, there to be "shared" with the person or deity being honored, then returned home for final preparation.

One of the earliest celebrations of the year, just about a month after the Lantern Festival, honored Kwan Yin, the revered Goddess of Mercy, also looked upon as a goddess of womanhood. Ah Paw would pray all day to her, fingering her wooden beads, as we prepared a totally vegetarian meal, the highlight of which was her favorite feast in a dish, Buddha's Delight.

In the middle of the next month, March, we honored the death of Ah Paw's husband, Ah Gung, whom I never knew. He had been a wealthy landowner, scholar and a respected mandarin, who had died at an early age. A short while after his death, his and Ah Paw's only son had died as well and, as is Chinese custom, their lives were marked with a family banquet, for Ah Paw believed that they were still with us as spirits. Though it was a day of sad memories, it was as well a celebration of their lives, which is the way Ah Paw wished it.

On the anniversary my grandmother would pray constantly for much of the day, for her departed husband and son, sitting in front of her living room altar upon which rested a traditional altar ornament, a carved wood bar called a *sun chiu pa*, its face etched, and gold-filled, with the names of her husband and son. She would ask these ancestors, who were surely in heaven, to bless the remainder of their family and intercede with the gods to confer upon us all a safe journey through a long life. Throughout the day, the servants cooked and I helped, and as each dish was completed it would be brought to Ah Gung's altar, offered, then returned to the kitchen.

In the afternoon, one or more of those Buddhist nuns whom Ah Paw had adopted as friends would come to her house and chant prayers in the memory of Ah Gung. Two banquet dishes were always prepared for this family observance, both using that special treat, Chinese bacon, then available only in the cooler early months. More important, both dishes had been favorites of my grandfather when he was alive.

Boiled Pork

(Bo Chi Yuk)

This basic dish, made with fresh Chinese bacon, was a favorite of Ah Paw's and a recurring festive offering. It is called *ng far yuk*, or "five flower meat," to describe its half-fat, half-lean texture. Fresh Chinese bacon is quite flavorful when boiled, but should there be a desire for leaner meat, this dish can also be made with a two-pound piece of lean pork loin.

1 piece 2¼- to 2½-pound fresh Chinese bacon, left whole

6 cups cold water

2 teaspoons salt

3 scallions, trimmed, cut into thirds

½ cup coriander, coarsely cut into 3-inch pieces

In a large pot place all ingredients, making certain water covers meat completely. Bring to a boil, uncovered, over high heat. Lower heat, cover pot and simmer for 30 to 45 minutes, until pork is tender. Test by pushing a chopstick into the lean meat; it should go in easily. Turn off heat, allow pork to rest in liquid for 20 minutes. Drain, discard solids and retain liquid.

It was our custom to save the liquid and to use it to reheat the pork after it had been offered whole at Ah Paw's altar. To reheat, place pork in liquid, bring to a boil and cook until hot, about 5 minutes. Remove from liquid, allow to cool, slice thinly and arrange on a platter. Serve with soy sauce poured into individual soy sauce dishes.

SERVES 4 TO 6

Stir-Fried Glutinous Rice

(Sang Chau Nor Mai Fan)

生炒糯米飯

Because of its many ingredients, this very special dish is considered to be a dish of honor that warms the body. It is made with cured Chinese bacon, which is cured with thick soy sauce, rice wine, salt and white pepper. It comes in slabs, usually about 8 ounces each. It will keep refrigerated, for at least 2 months.

2 cups glutinous rice

2 cups cold water

8 cups boiling water

½ cup cured Chinese bacon, cut into ¼-inch dice

½ cup Chinese sausage (*lop cheung*), cut into ¼-inch dice

2 tablespoons dried shrimp, soaked in hot water 30 minutes to soften

¾ teaspoon salt

1 teaspoon light soy sauce

1 teaspoon dark soy sauce

2 tablespoons oyster sauce

3 scallions, finely sliced

2 teaspoons sesame oil

In a pot, wash, rinse the glutinous rice three times by rubbing between the palms, drain well. Place rice in a 9-inch cake pan and add 2 cups cold water. Place pan in a steamer, on a rack. Place rack in wok, turn heat to high, pour in 8 cups boiling water, cover and steam rice, 30 to 35 minutes, or until rice becomes translucent (see steaming directions, page 30). Remove steamer from wok, set aside, drain wok, wash and dry.

Heat wok over high heat for 45 seconds. Put in bacon, stir-fry 30 seconds, push to one side. Add sausage, stir-fry 1 minute, then combine sausage and bacon. Add shrimp, stir-fry 15 seconds, add salt and stir another 15 seconds. Add steamed rice to wok and lower heat, mixing continually for 1 more minute. If rice sticks, add 1½ tablespoons peanut oil. Add two soy sauces, mix thoroughly. Add oyster sauce, stir until rice acquires an even, pale brown color and is thoroughly mixed. Add scallions, mix well. Turn off heat, add sesame oil and mix to combine well.

Pack the cooked rice into small bowls, then up-end them onto plates to create curved mounds of rice. Serve immediately.

SERVES 4 TO 6

THE FESTIVAL OF CHING MING, or "going to the graves," came in the fourth month, 106 days after the end of the New Year observance, usually near the end of April or the beginning of May. Though widely celebrated as a public holiday throughout China, it was intensely personal as well. It was a time reserved for visiting the graves of one's ancestors, sweeping their graves clean and presenting them with symbolic foods.

In Sah Gau there were no graveyards, no headstones in the usual sense. All of those who had passed away were buried on family-owned plots of land—in Ah Paw's case, on a small hill overlooking her rice and sugarcane fields. The gravesite was marked by a half-moon ridge of earth, a backdrop for the pyramid of earth that marked the burial place of her husband and son. Atop the pyramid were two thick circles of sod, the first placed grass-side down atop the pyramid, the second, grass-side up, resting upon the first. Each year these two pieces were replaced to refresh the graves, then the dirt was swept neatly.

The servants, Ah Guk and Sau Lin, and I, would begin cooking early in the morning and in the afternoon walk to the graves on the outskirts of Sah Gau. Ah Paw, because of her bound feet, would not make the journey, but would pray at her altar while we cleaned the grave and made our food offerings.

We would bring white cut chicken, boiled pork, often a whole fish and a vegetarian dish such as Buddha's Delight as well as three bowls of rice, three pairs of chopsticks, three cups of wine and three cups of tea. Small amounts of tea and wine were poured on the ground at the foot of the earth pyramid, so that those buried could "drink." Then each of the prepared dishes would be tipped forward at the pyramid so they could "eat," these followed by similarly tipping bowls full of oranges, tangerines and grapefruit. Candles we had brought would be lighted, incense would be burned. Gold- and silver-embossed white paper money we had brought would also be burned so that those in heaven would have some wealth, some comfort. We would then return home with our food, where the chicken would be cut up, the pork sliced, the Buddha's Delight tossed, then all served, cold, out of respect for the dead.

Throughout the year there were weddings and births, always times for happy family gatherings, for celebratory banquets. In the years I spent visiting and learning in my grandmother's kitchen, only male cousins from Ah Paw's side of the family were married. This being the circumstance, she always gave an informal, but special, dinner about a week before the wedding, just for the prospective groom and his family. There were no particular rituals, just a gathering to eat and to wish my cousin well.

Because I was so young at the time, I recall asking Ah Paw if only boys were given banquets. No, Ah Fei, she said. If I am alive when you marry, you will have a wonderful banquet. As it turned out, when I was married, my Ah Paw had passed away a long time earlier, but I recall telling my husband that he should thank Ah Paw, silently, for what we both thought was a fine wedding party.

The parties Ah Paw threw before weddings were large affairs, too large for her modest house, so they were held in one of the other houses left in her care by her husband. We always served familiar, favorite dishes such as Five-Spice Kau Yuk, Fish Alive raw fish, congees, barbecued suckling pig and always an eagerly anticipated banquet heirloom, the very special Salt-Baked Chicken and all manner of won tons and other noodles.

Won Ton

(WON TON)

No noodle is more famous than the won ton. Though often regarded as a dumpling, the won ton is actually a filled noodle, most often stuffed with pork and shrimp, and served as a first course for such celebrations as this pre-wedding dinner. The skins would be bought at the market in Sah Gau. When I was learning to make won ton, we always made them to eat in the same day because without refrigeration the shrimp and pork filling could not be allowed to rest overnight in our generally warm climate.

FILLING

12 ounces lean pork, ground

4 ounces shrimp (about 8 large shrimp), shelled, deveined and finely diced

1½ cups scallions, finely sliced

1½ teaspoons minced garlic

1 tablespoon grated ginger

4 water chestnuts, peeled, finely diced, or ¼ cup jicama, finely diced

1 tablespoon Chinese white rice wine, or gin

2 egg whites, lightly beaten

1 teaspoon salt

1 teaspoon sugar

1 teaspoon light soy sauce

1 teaspoon sesame oil

1½ tablespoons oyster sauce

Pinch white pepper

36 won ton skins

3½ tablespoons cornstarch

10 cups cold water

1 tablespoon salt

1 tablespoon peanut oil

Mix together all the filling ingredients, until thoroughly blended. Place in a shallow dish, refrigerate, uncovered, 4 hours, or covered overnight.

MAKE THE WON TON: Skins should be kept at room temperature. Work with one at a time, keeping remainder under a damp towel. Keep a bowl of water at hand to wet edges of skins. Place 1 tablespoon of filling in center of a won ton skin, wet edges, fold in half and seal edges. Wet the folded corners, not the sealed corners, and draw ends together to create a bow-like dumpling, like a tortellini. Repeat until 36 won ton are made. As each is made, place on a cookie sheet dusted with cornstarch.

Place water, salt and peanut oil in a pot, cover and bring to a boil over high heat. Add won ton, stir and cook for about 8 minutes until won ton are translucent, and filling can be seen through the skin. Turn off heat, run cold water into pot, drain. Serve immediately. Leftover won ton should be placed on wax paper to dry thoroughly before refrigerating for later use.

MAKES 36 WON TON

Salt-Baked Chicken

(Guangdong Yim Guk Gai)

Salt-baked chicken, in which a whole chicken is essentially baked in an "oven" of salt that encloses it, is a recipe of southern China, a dish loved by the native Cantonese as well as their historic "visitor people," the Hakka migrants to Guangdong. Our family's version differed in ingredients. In Ah Paw's kitchen we added cloves, anise seeds, and a fermented rose petal spirit, and enclosed the chicken in a strong parchment we called *sah ji*, or "sandpaper." Baking the chicken in its salt cover does not make it salty, but instead it keeps it moist.

In my grandmother's kitchen, the chicken, covered with salt, sat in a wok covered with a wooden wok cover, and was cooked atop a stove over a wood fire. This dish surely fit Ah Paw's description of a dish that would take a good deal of effort to make, and would show that effort.

Today I cook it, and teach it, differently because we have ovens. It is easier and more simple to make Salt-Baked Chicken in the modern manner. The parchment available these days is not as thick and strong as the Chinese "sandpaper," so I wrap the chicken in lotus leaves instead, or in two yards of cheesecloth.

5 pounds kosher salt

1 3-pound whole chicken

MARINADE

¾ teaspoon salt

½ teaspoon cloves (about 12)

⅛ teaspoon anise seeds

1½ tablespoons Mei Kuei Lu Chiew rose petal spirit, or gin

3 scallions, trimmed, cut in half across, white portions lightly smashed

1 slice ginger, ½ inch thick, lightly smashed

1 tablespoon dark soy sauce

2 lotus leaves, soaked in hot water 10 minutes, until soft and pliable, rinsed and drained

HEAT THE SALT: Place half the salt in a Dutch oven, half in a roasting pan. Place both in an oven heated to 375 degrees F, for 40 minutes until salt is very hot.

AS THE SALT HEATS, PREPARE CHICKEN: Clean and wash chicken, removing all fat and membranes. Sprinkle chicken with ¼ cup salt, rub well into the bird, rinse under cold water, drain, pat dry with paper towels. Mix the marinade (¾ teaspoon salt, cloves, anise seed and rose petal spirit) in a small bowl. Rub the cavity of the chicken with the mixture, to coat well, then pour remainder into the cavity. Place scallions and ginger in cavity, skewer the opening closed. Rub outside of chicken with soy sauce to coat evenly.

WRAP THE CHICKEN: Lay lotus leaves on flat surface, overlapping slightly. Place chicken breast-side up in center. Fold leaves up over the sides of chicken, then bring up the ends to cover. The pliable leaves should stay in place.

Remove salt from oven. Spread salt in Dutch oven to create a well. Place chicken, breast-side up, in the well. Pour remainder of salt over the chicken to completely cover. Place Dutch oven in 375 degree F oven and bake for 20 minutes. Lower heat to 350 degrees F, bake another 30 minutes. Turn off oven, allow chicken to rest in oven for 5 minutes more. The chicken should be baked perfectly at this point. Take chicken from oven and allow to cool 10 minutes.

Remove wrapped chicken from salt, remove lotus leaves, place chicken on a chopping board. Cut into bite-size pieces. Serve with individual small dishes of soy sauce.

SERVES 4 TO 6

NOTE Unfortunately, this classic dish is often misrepresented. Beware the common inauthentic, pallid imitation of this great historical preparation. Instead of baking a chicken in salt, the bird is often cooked in a heated salt solution, thus making it nothing more than simply a salty, boiled chicken.

WHEN THERE WERE WEDDINGS THERE WERE, in the customary order of things, births. Much was, and is, made of babies in China. There are special dishes to be eaten by women after they have given birth, and different special dishes to celebrate these births.

The first meal a woman eats after giving birth is traditionally a plain fried rice tossed with shreds of gingerroot. This is to instantly begin the process of rebuilding the blood, and giving constant warmth to the body. Directly after that came a period of recurring meals of Boy's Birth Vinegar, prepared with great zeal when a boy was born.

Boy's Birth Vinegar

(Tim Ding Tim Cho)

溱
丁
甜
醋

This dish is named unequally, in my view. Its name, *tim ding tim cho*, translates as "sweet vinegar for the birth of a son." I remember asking my grandmother why girls did not have their own sweet vinegar. Her reply, quite simply, was *"Daw see, daw see,"* or "You ask too many questions." She then added that it was for girls, too. That did not really satisfy me, but I kept quiet, because I loved eating it.

This dish was usually made in three-day batches: three days, three meals each day, two eggs each meal, to be eaten every day for one month. During this month, the woman who has given birth will eat the birth vinegar regularly, and only small amounts of pork or fish, with some vegetables, nothing more. When it was made in Ah Paw's house for her first great-grandson, it was made in vast amounts, because it was meant to be shared with any neighbor who dropped in, carrying an envelope of lucky money in one hand, an empty bowl in the other. In fact, her neighbors would drop by repeatedly, while the vinegar was cooking, to ask when it would be done.

The mixture is strong, and is regarded as a medicine, for females only. However, my memory is that quite a few men ate it as well.

> 3 pounds young ginger, peeled, cut into 2½-inch pieces, each lightly smashed
>
> 4 28-oz. bottles thick, sweet, black Chinese rice vinegar
>
> 4 pounds pigs' feet, cut into 2-inch pieces
>
> ¾ pound sugarcane sugar, or dark brown sugar
>
> 18 peeled hard-boiled eggs

Place ginger, sweet vinegar and pigs' feet in a large pot. Cover, bring to a boil over high heat. Reduce heat to simmer, leaving pot lid open slightly and simmer, 3½ hours. Stir from time to time with a wooden spoon. The pigs' feet should be tender. Taste the vinegar. It should taste balanced, between sweet and tart. Variations will occur because of differences in batches of rice vinegars. Add sugar to taste, cook until melted and blended. Add hard-boiled eggs, stir, make certain eggs are completely immersed in liquid. Simmer for another 30 minutes. Turn off heat, serve immediately with cooked rice.

MAKES APPROXIMATELY 18 SERVINGS

AT BIRTH, ALL NEWBORN CHILDREN—*ah mui*, baby girls, or *ah jai*, baby boys—are given what are called "milk names," to indicate that they will not have proper names while they are quite young and still drinking milk. I was told that my milk name was Bibi Noi, or simply Little Baby. Nor did I receive my "ginger name," or given name, for several months until my father, who was away, sent his choice of name for me, Yin-Fei, to our family. A so-called pen name, self-chosen, is usually not taken until a child begins school, but I kept using Yin-Fei until I went to Hong Kong, where I took the English name of Eileen for myself because I thought it sounded pretty in front of Yin-Fei.

When a baby reached one month in age, there was always a banquet marking the occasion, for it was on that day she, or he, received his, or her, given, or ginger, name. I was an exception, not receiving my ginger name for several months, but Ah Paw said that it did not matter because she had prayed earnestly to the nine female goddesses who protect children to keep watch over me.

Praying to them was powerful, Ah Paw would say, telling me repeatedly how her prayers had protected her grandson, Ah Mui, from death, allowing her to outwit a jealous god who wanted to take her grandson. Ah Mui was my only cousin for some time. He had been born to my number-two aunt, who had two earlier boys die in infancy. She, and her mother-in-law, Ah Paw, were convinced that the baby boys had been stolen and killed by a jealous god.

Ah Paw was determined that this would not happen again, so she prayed to Yin Meng, a goddess charged with protecting babies from falling and being hurt. Her strategy, which she was convinced had come directly from Yin Meng, was to deceive the jealous god by declaring Ah Mui a girl, despite his having been born a male. Thus his name, Ah Mui, or Baby Girl. He was called this throughout his life. Even after he was later given a male name, Cheong Yeun, he was known always as Ah Mui in our family even after he married and had his own family.

Ah Paw would tell me this story before every banquet commemorating a baby's first month. It gave her pleasure to believe that a mortal had been able to fool a god. A happy tale to accompany a banquet for a one-month-old, that always included red dyed eggs, for good luck, at least one dish of noodles, ginger pickle and steamed fish, and the centerpiece of the observance, Guangfu Chicken.

Guangfu Chicken

(JAH JI GAI)

This classic dish was always part of this family feast celebrating a child's first month since birth. Its name, Guangfu, translates as "the dish of the Guangdong people," and like all traditional, elegant chicken dishes, connoted the concept of birth. As with other desirable dishes, it is time-consuming to make, but I always enjoyed the effort when I shared my grandmother's kitchen making it with her servants, and I continue to enjoy it today. We used a special spice for this chicken called *cho guah;* the closest approximation is nutmeg.

1 3-pound whole chicken

¼ cup salt

CHICKEN COATING

1½ tablespoons honey melted with 2 tablespoons boiling water

1 tablespoon Shao-Hsing wine, or sherry

1 teaspoon Chinese white rice vinegar, or distilled white vinegar

½ teaspoon cornstarch

3 pieces 8-star anise

½ whole dried tangerine peel

3 cinnamon sticks, 2 inches long

1 slice ginger, 1 inch thick, lightly smashed

10 cups cold water

2 tablespoons salt

2 tablespoons sugar

¼ cup Chinese white rice wine, or gin

1 whole nutmeg

6 cups peanut oil, for deep-frying

PREPARE THE CHICKEN: Clean, remove all fat and membranes and wash with cold water. Sprinkle ¼ cup salt on outside of chicken, rub well into the skin, rinse under cold running water and drain well. Mix coating ingredients, reserve.

In a large pot combine all ingredients from anise to nutmeg and bring to a boil over high heat. Cover pot, lower heat and simmer for 20 minutes. Turn heat to high, bring to a boil again. Place chicken in pot, breast side up, cover. When pot begins to boil, lower heat immediately, simmer for 10 minutes. Turn chicken over, repeat process. Turn off heat, allow chicken to sit for 10 minutes with pot covered. Remove chicken, discard all ingredients from pot. Place chicken on a rack over a large platter to drain. As it drains, pierce chicken with a cooking fork to help process. Drain 1 to 1½ hours.

With a pastry brush coat chicken thoroughly with coating mixture. Allow coated chicken to dry thoroughly, about 6 hours. (The use of an electric fan can cut this drying period in half.) As it dries, turn the chicken several times, taking care not to disturb the coating.

Heat wok over high heat 1 minute, add peanut oil, heat to 375 degrees F. Using a large Chinese strainer, lower chicken into the oil, breast side up and deep-fry 3 minutes. Ladle over chicken to ensure uniformity of frying. Turn chicken over by inserting a wooden spoon in its cavity and fry for another 3 minutes, ladling oil as before. Repeat until chicken is golden brown. Turn off heat, remove chicken, allow to drain. Place on chopping board and chop into bite-size pieces. Serve immediately with Roasted Spice Salt.

SERVES 4 TO 6

Roasted Spice Salt

2 teaspoons salt

½ teaspoon five-spice powder

½ teaspoon whole Sichuan peppercorns

Heat wok over high heat 45 seconds. Lower heat to low medium, add all ingredients. Dry-roast, stirring, until five-spice powder turns black. Remove, strain off peppercorns, discard them. Place spice salt in a small dish and serve with chicken.

TUEN NG, THE FESTIVAL OF THE Dragon Boats, is a significant celebration that involves much of China, particularly in cities and towns along its southeastern shores, and where there are sizable bays, rivers and lakes. Within China, Tuen Ng is a national holiday that involves competitions among hundreds of ornate dragon boats. Outside of China, it is an observance with which many westerners are familiar.

It is a holiday rooted in mythology that occurs in late May or early June and is said to commemorate Qu Yuan, a Chinese patriot of the fourth century B.C., a poet and scholar who, to draw attention to the corruption in his country, drowned himself in protest. He either lost the confidence of his emperor or was forced from his position of scholarship by corrupt officials, but whatever his circumstance, he wrote a series of poems that expressed his sorrow, but also his love for his country and its people.

People raced to the river in a vain effort to save him. They slapped at the water with their oars to frighten away any fish that might come to feed on him, and threw rice dumplings wrapped in silk into the waters to give him sustenance and honor. The Dragon Boat Festival annually honors Qu Yuan, and appeases the great dragon who controls the waters, so that there will be sufficient rainfall and well-irrigated fields to ensure abundant crops.

This tale is memorialized in rowing competitions up and down China, with each town or municipality entering brightly painted longboats, with carved dragon heads jutting upward from their bows. The paddlers move in perfect unison, and prizes are awarded to the winners. In recent years there have even been boats entered from the United States and other western countries. In both Siu Lo Chun, my village, and Sah Gau, Ah Paw's town, I loved to watch the dragon boat teams as they trained for weeks before the festival.

Because it was a national holiday, we would have a banquet that would see roasted suckling pig at our table, along with Guangfu Chicken, quite a bit of seafood such as shrimp and crab, and certainly a steamed fish. But the one food we had to have were *cheong*, glutinous rice dumplings with a variety of fillings. They were small pyramids of steamed glutinous rice filled with salted duck eggs, pork, chestnuts or red bean paste.

The most famous of these traditional dumplings were *ham yuk cheong*, stuffed with a mix of pork, chicken, mung beans and salted duck egg yolks and wrapped tightly with fresh bamboo leaves, then poached in boiling water. It was perfectly named "for all," since we all shared in it. However, these delicacies were just an introduction to our Dragon Boat evening banquet, the centerpiece of which was a grand dish of tradition, Lo Soi Duck.

Lo Soi Duck

(Lo Soi Op)

What is important with this preparation is the sauce, the lo soi, a master sauce, constantly replenished, used for months and years, a sauce without end. The literal translation of the words *lo soi* is "old water," which describes it perfectly, if not with the elegance it deserves. Once a duck is cooked in lo soi, that sauce becomes the sauce for the next duck, and so on. Ah Paw had a lo soi in her kitchen that had been there for many, many years. Each day, at her order, it was brought to a boil to preserve it, keep it potent and to ensure its longevity. Occasionally flavors and spices were added to it. Once a duck had been cooked in it, the remaining sauce, the new lo soi, could be used to cook two to three additional ducks, without any additional ingredients. To this day, master chefs throughout China guard their lo soi, even passing them on to their successors.

4 pieces 8-star anise

4 cinnamon sticks, each 3 inches long

½ tablespoon fennel seed

½ teaspoon Sichuan peppercorns

½ dried tangerine peel

6 pieces licorice root, each 1½ inches long

1 whole nutmeg

½ teaspoon whole cloves

1 piece ginger, 2 inches long lightly smashed

4 cloves garlic, peeled

3 scallions, each cut into 3-inch pieces

5 cups cold water

5 cups Chicken Stock (page 13)

2 cups dark soy sauce

2 cups light soy sauce

1 pound rock sugar, or light brown sugar

¾ cup Mei Kuei Lu Chiew rose petal spirit, or gin

1 5- to 5½-pound freshly killed duck

¼ cup salt

PREPARE A SMALL SPICE PILLOW: Fold a 10-inch square piece of cheese-cloth in half, then half again, to create a 5-inch square. Sew 2 of the 3 open sides closed. Place all ingredients from 8-star anise to scallions in the pillow and sew it closed.

PREPARE THE LO SOI: In a large pot place cold water, stock and spice pillow and bring to a boil over high heat. Add two soy sauces, return to a boil. Add sugar, stir to dissolve and return to a boil. Add rose spirit and return to a boil. Lower heat, simmer for 1 hour, covered, leaving a small opening at the lid.

WHILE THE LO SOI SIMMERS, PREPARE THE DUCK: Wash it thoroughly inside cavity and out and remove membranes. Rub ¼ cup salt over duck, rinse off, drain well. Cut off first two joints of both wings, discard.

Place a cake rack in the pot. Lower duck, breast side down, onto rack. Turn heat to high and bring lo soi back to a boil. Lower heat immediately and simmer duck, covered for 2 hours, if head is on; 1½ hours if head is off. Ladle sauce over duck periodically if it is not completely covered. Make certain heat is low, so the duck skin will not split. Turn off heat. Allow duck to rest in the lo soi for 1 hour, to fully absorb the sauce. Remove to a cutting board, cut into bite-size pieces, remove to a heated platter and serve immediately. The lo soi may be kept indefinitely, refrigerated. I recommend bringing to a boil at least every 2 months.

SERVES 4 TO 6

WE CELEBRATED A MORE GENTLE FESTIVAL very soon after the Dragon Festival, as the year edged into August, a feast celebrating love and marriage instead of revenge. The Maiden's Festival, or more familiarly, The Feast of the Seven Sisters, was observed by young, unmarried women. Its mythology is sweet, and tells the tale of two young lovers, a cow herder and a fairy, who became separated by the gods, and were forced to live on separate stars. The birds of the air took pity on them, however, and once a year the birds flew in unison, creating a heavenly bridge with their outstretched wings, which enabled the lovers to meet between their stars.

It was a lovely story, told to me repeatedly by Ah Paw, and celebrated in a quiet way. Offerings of fruit were made to the gods in heaven, along with paper flowers and money, burnt to send upward. In particular, Ah Paw urged, I should pray to, and offer oranges to, the goddess P'ei Ku, who could, it was believed, make women beautiful, accomplished and desirable as wives.

Ah Paw saw to it that I ate only fruit on this day, as was the custom for young and unmarried women, and talked to me of future husbands. She would pick up a pair of chopsticks, hold them low, closer to the ends that picked up food, then slide her hand back so that she was holding them far to the tops. If I held my chopsticks close to the bottom, Ah Paw said, I would marry a husband close to where I lived. If I held them near the tops, I would marry a man from far away. I do not remember exactly how I held my chopsticks then, but it must have been near the top.

September was an important month in our family, for two birthdays occurred in it: those of Confucius and my grandmother, Ah Paw.

Confucius was most important to Ah Paw. Though she was a religious Buddhist, much of her manners and morality, her behavior toward others and her attitudes regarding social order came from the Analects of Confucius, which she would repeat to me often as lessons, more so on his birthday. Confucius was a simple man, she would say, who when asked his opinion of war he said he knew more about preparing meat for his lunch than he did about war.

Much of what she taught me had to do with Confucius and food, with food as a constant metaphor for other aspects of life. He was the simplest of men, she said, who thought so much of food, its tastes and preparations that he would specify precisely how foods ought to be cut before cooking. He was nevertheless content with "a small amount of dried meat," and happy with "plain food to eat and pure water to drink."

Confucius desired rice to be at its whitest, meat finely diced or sliced. If food was overcooked, he would not eat it. If fish or meat had lost their color, he would not eat it. If food had what he thought was a distasteful odor, he would not eat it. He insisted, Ah Paw said, that food be eaten in season, not be preserved, and that sauces served with food should enhance it, not change its nature. He would sip a bit of wine out of politeness, but "would have no meal that did not have some ginger."

We would eat simply on Confucius's birthday, a meal of rice and vegetables, and of a dish that Ah Paw believed Confucius would have liked for its felicitous assortment of ingredients.

Dragon and Phoenix Soup

(Lung Fung Tong)

This soup is symbolic as well, the lobster, or "dragon shrimp," representing the emperor, the chicken, or the phoenix, a representation of the empress. It is also a symbol of a happy marriage, and was served as part of a wedding day banquet. Ah Paw thought it just fine for Confucius's birthday, and it was served annually on the occasion. Incidentally, the soup was considered incomplete if it did not contain the "dragon's whiskers," or bean threads.

MARINADES

(Mix 2 identical marinades as below, one for chicken, one for lobster)

1½ teaspoons ginger juice

1 tablespoon Chinese white rice wine, or gin

1 teaspoon light soy sauce

¾ teaspoon salt

¾ teaspoon sugar

1 teaspoon sesame oil

Pinch white pepper

½ teaspoon Chinese white rice vinegar, or distilled white vinegar

2 teaspoons cornstarch

12 ounces chicken cutlets, trimmed of fat and membranes, cut into ½-inch dice

2 lobster tails, about 1 pound each, shelled, deveined, washed, dried and cut into ½-inch dice

3 cups peanut oil

1 ounce bean threads (half package)

5 cups Chicken Stock (page 13)

1 tablespoon minced ginger

2 cloves garlic, minced

½ cup fresh mushrooms, cut into ½-inch dice

½ cup bamboo shoots, cut into ⅓-inch dice

½ cup fresh peas (or frozen, allow to defrost)

3 egg whites, beaten

¼ cup scallions, finely sliced

Marinade chicken and lobster in their individual marinade. Allow to rest 30 minutes each and reserve.

Heat wok over high heat 40 seconds, add peanut oil, coat wok with spatula. When a wisp of white smoke appears, add bean threads. These cook immediately, so have a strainer ready and pick them out of the wok with a strainer in 5 seconds. Drain and reserve.

Pour chicken stock into a pot, add ginger and garlic, cover and bring to a boil over high heat. Add mushrooms and bamboo shoots, cover, return to a boil and allow to cook 2 minutes. Add peas, return to a boil. Add chicken and its marinade, stir to combine, return to a boil. Cook for 2 minutes, until chicken turns white. Add lobster and its marinade, stir. Add beaten eggs, mix gently with a ladle to permit eggs to blend. Add bean threads, stir. Add scallions, mix briefly. Turn off heat, pour into a heated tureen and serve immediately.

SERVES 4 TO 6

AH PAW'S BIRTHDAY CAME SOON AFTER, in September, and in her house it was a day of prayer, of wishing her well, with a series of special greetings, as the head of our family, finally preparing for her a dish of honor. I would turn over in her bed, hug her, and whisper, *"Juk Nei Sahng Sun Fai Lok,"* simply, "I wish you a happy birthday." My reward was a smile and a return hug,

On the morning of her birthday we ate no breakfast, for Ah Paw desired a small fast, before eating one bowl of a simple congee at lunch. She would then be carried to her big living room chair, in front of her ancestor altar. A pillow would be set at her feet and all of us in our family would kneel to her, offer her a cup of tea and extend our greetings, in order. First to kneel were my two aunts. Each gave her a cup of tea, each said, *"Kung hei sun tai ghin hong,"* or "Congratulations and good health."

My mother was next. Her words were *"Sum seung yue ee,"* or "Whatever you are thinking of will come true." My brother, who knelt next, said, *"Sau bei lam san,"* or "Your life is as vast as the Southern Mountain," a sentiment repeated by my cousin. I then knelt and wished her the same happy birthday as I had earlier, handing her a cup of tea. With each cup of tea, she would pour a few drops in front of her altar to share her tea with her deceased husband, then give each of us an envelope of lucky money. She always gave to others on her birthday. This included her servants, who were the last to kneel before her, after which they, my aunts and I went off to the kitchen to prepare Ah Paw's birthday meal.

And quite special it was: a shark's fin soup that was said to clear and regenerate one's skin; a sweet soup of birds' nest, to keep one's complexion youthful; *sau bau*, so-called birthday buns shaped like peaches, the symbols of a long life; a steamed fish and her favorite chicken.

Grandmother's Birthday Chicken

(Jo Moh Sang Yat Gai)

外婆生日鷄

This unusual and festive chicken, cooked in soy sauce, was always prepared for Ah Paw's birthday. It was considered a dish of honor, one celebrating her position as family matriarch. Cooking this dish produces another of those "master sauces," *see yau*. Once made it can be used to cook chicken again and again. On my grandmother's birthday, hard-boiled eggs and the chicken's liver and gizzards were often added to the sauce in her honor. Each time the sauce was used, additional seasonings were added, and the *see yau* became more complex and richer with age. These sauces are never discarded. In fact, I have one in my kitchen to this day.

4 cups Chicken Stock (page 13)

2 cups cold water

3 cinnamon sticks, each 3 inches long

4 whole pieces 8-star anise

1 slice ginger, 2 inches thick lightly smashed

5 ounces sugarcane sugar, or brown sugar

1 cup double dark soy sauce

1 cup Shao-Hsing wine, or sherry

1 3½-pound whole chicken, thoroughly washed, cleaned inside and out, rubbed with ¼ cup salt and rinsed

In a large pot, place chicken stock, water, cinnamon, star anise, ginger and sugar, cover and bring to a boil over high heat. Add soy sauce, return to a boil. Lower heat, cover pot, allow sauce to simmer 20 minutes. Return heat to high, add wine, return to a boil. Lower chicken, breast-side up, into liquid and return to a boil. Lower heat, cover pot and simmer for 20 minutes. Turn chicken over, simmer for another 20 minutes. Turn off heat and allow chicken to rest in liquid, covered, for 1 hour.

Transfer to a cutting board, cut chicken into bite-size pieces and serve immediately.

SERVES 4 TO 6

NOTE The *see yau* may be saved for future use. Strain into a container and refrigerate. It will keep 2 to 3 months, and be a perfect base for cooking this chicken again. If you do this, add a little of each ingredient to the mix.

AT THE END OF HER BIRTHDAY party, Ah Paw always had a small lesson, one that stressed respect and honor for elders, family or otherwise. "The older one becomes, the more respect should be shown," she would say. And she would point out that with age came experience and knowledge. "Always remember that an older person has eaten more grains of salt than you have eaten grains of rice," she would say before sending me off to bed.

The national feast of the Autumn Moon, or Jung Chau Chit, is celebrated with one of China's more enduring sweet, the moon cake. The festival, which centers upon the moon and its mythology, goes back more than 1,500 years to the time of the Tang Dynasty. It is said that a heavenly archer, as a reward for shooting down nine of the ten scourges besetting the earth, was given an herb of immortality. His wife found the herb, ate it, then fearing the anger of her husband, fled to the moon. She arrived breathless and choking, and coughed up the herb, which landed on the moon, becoming a jade rabbit upon impact. On the night of the Autumn Moon people walk the streets carrying elaborate lighted paper lanterns, and search the sky for the full moon, on which they are certain can be seen the image of that good luck rabbit.

The moon cakes, or *yeut bang*, date as far back as the festival itself. These cakes, of heavy sweet fillings, such as lotus seed or red bean pastes, often with nuts, around cooked salted duck egg yolks, and covered with a thin layer of wheat flour dough, can be obtained only at this time of the year. Bakeries work feverishly to make sufficient amounts of them, and call attention to the number of yolks they contain: the more yolks, the more expensive and, the luckier. At Ah Paw's house we never made these because of the great effort needed, and because they were so plentiful in the town bakeries. But we bought many, many boxes of them, for ourselves and for visitors, and ate them to excess for their overly sweet richness.

To this day I buy them by the box each October and eat them with great enjoyment, telling myself that I am faithfully observing the Autumn Moon Festival.

Our family's observance of the Winter Solstice was celebrated at home. It was, and is, very much a Chinese version of Thanksgiving, a happy time remembering with pleasure good harvests of the past year. Temple offerings were made to Shen Nung, the God of Agriculture, in hopes that he would again smile upon our fields and crops in the coming year. Known commonly as Lop Dong, or the beginning of winter, the dinner we ate in thanksgiving was substantial, and included some of the favorite dishes of Ah Paw's household. Because the weather had cooled by this time, we were able to obtain dishes denied us in summer months, such as salted pork, fresh or cured bacon and *lop cheong*, pork and pork liver sausages, and of course Ah Paw's favorite, Buddha's Delight, and a thick cake of glutinous rice studded with candied fruit called 8-Treasure Rice.

Part of our Winter Solstice feast was always the communal hot pot.

Hot Pot

(Dah Bin Lo)

The preparation known as the hot pot exists throughout China, in many guises. Its name, *dah bin lo*, translates loosely as "gathering around the table," and connotes a central dish of boiling broth in which meats and fish are cooked in small bits to be eaten communally. In Ah Paw's house this was a most festive dish, reserved only for the winter because it was so warming.

A small portable clay stove, fired by charcoal, was brought from the kitchen to the dining table. Over its flame was placed a clay pot of boiling water with ginger and scallions, in which we cooked our foods. As with other special dishes from Ah Paw's kitchen, this required some work, but the enjoyment far outweighed the effort.

1 pound pork loin, cut in half lengthwise, then sliced into thin half-moons

¾ pound chicken cutlets, thinly sliced

1 pound shrimp (about 20) shelled, deveined and washed

1 pound filet sea bass, thinly sliced

1 pound spinach, old leaves discarded, stalks separated, washed 3 or 4 times to remove grit, drained

1 bunch mum greens (1 pound) washed, drained and stems removed (or cabbage, cut into 1-inch by 3-inch sections)

2 bunches watercress, washed, drained

4 ounces (2 packages) bean thread noodles soaked in hot water 15 minutes until soft, cut into 6-inch strands

4 cakes firm bean curd, cut into ¼-inch slices

8 cups cold water

1 piece ginger, 1½ inch thick, lightly smashed

4 scallions, trimmed, cut into 2-inch sections

2 teaspoons salt

4 tablespoons peanut oil

Prepare meats, vegetables, bean thread noodles and bean curd, arrange in individual dishes around a portable stove that will hold a large pot. (An electric fry pan will substitute well.) Place water, ginger, scallions, salt and peanut oil in a large pot. Bring to a boil over high heat. Lower heat to simmer for 10 minutes, then bring pot to the table and place on portable stove.

At this point you may eat as eclectically as you wish, placing whichever meat, fish, seafood, bean curd or vegetable of your choice into the broth and cooking it. I recommend using small, strainerlike spoons fashioned of wire, which are available in Asian markets. Or you may use slotted spoons. Accompany what you eat with either or both of the following dipping sauces.

Sesame Dip

4 tablespoons sesame seed paste

4 tablespoons light soy sauce

2 tablespoons Shao-Hsing wine, or sherry

1 tablespoon Chinese red rice vinegar, or red wine vinegar

1 tablespoon sugar

Vinegar Dip

2 tablespoons Chinese red rice vinegar, or red wine vinegar

4 tablespoons light soy sauce

1 tablespoon Chinese white rice wine, or gin

1 tablespoon minced ginger

1 tablespoon sugar

Combine ingredients for each sauce.

Divide dipping sauces into individual small soy sauce dishes, to serve.

SERVES UP TO 8

THE SOLSTICE WAS THE BEGINNING OF our winter, admittedly not very cold, but much cooler than the green, warm springs and summers, even autumns, of southern China. I had learned to cook the cooling foods of summer with Ah Paw, to steam papayas and pears, to double-boil squashes and melons, sweetening them with honey and dates. And winter brought its own rewards. I learned from Ah Paw of the heat that could be brought into the body with double-boiled pork soups, with stews and other dishes braised in the wok, of ginseng root boiled with chicken, of squabs roasted in a covered wok, and that peculiar breed of tough, black-fleshed chicken simmered for hours, so that only its flavor was left, the chicken discarded. And winter was notable as well because in just weeks Ah Paw would consult her Tung Sing and our busy New Year month would begin.

EIGHT

FROM GRANDMOTHER'S
HOUSE

FOR ALMOST SIX YEARS, UNTIL THE New Year of 1950, I had gone from my home in Siu Lo Chun to my grandmother's house in Sah Gah so often that it had become my second home. Thus it should not have been unexpected that, in that year in which I was to become twelve, when I decided to leave China, that I would depart from Ah Paw's house.

It was in that winter of 1949 that I made up my mind. I had been on school holiday for the New Year, spending most of my time, as usual, cooking in my grandmother's kitchen, helping her servants to primp her house. I decided I was not returning to school. I told Ah Paw of my choice. This reasonable woman did not, as I knew she wouldn't, suggest that I was being contrary. She simply asked me why.

I told her that at my school learning had stopped, that I and the other 350 students in our school spent little or no time in the classroom. Instead, we were walked from village to surrounding village where we danced and sang songs telling of the greatness of the People's Republic of China. By this time, after four years of civil war, Chiang Kai-Shek and his Kuomintang government had fled the mainland for Taiwan and the country was under the control of Mao Tze-Tung. We sang of that change of government, and of the revolution, and when we did go to our classrooms, it was to write letters to soldiers of the People's Liberation Army, praising them and telling them we appreciated their bravery.

I had already told my mother that school was a waste of time for me, that I did not intend to return, and that I wished to go to live with Ah Paw. My father was in Hong Kong at this time. My brother, Ching Moh, said that any decision was my own and agreed that I could go to my grandmother. He believed, I found out later, that after a visit to Ah Paw, I would choose to return home, and to school. So, when my grandmother asked my reasons, and I gave them to her, she nodded, agreed that I had made a good decision and said her home was of course mine, so long as I had decided not to return to school.

POSING WITH A FAMILY FRIEND'S PACKARD
SEDAN IN HONG KONG, 1950.

It was while I was in Sah Gau that I discovered that many people had fled, or were fleeing the town, and their country, for refuge in Hong Kong, then still an autonomous Crown Colony of Great Britain, which, it was said, was welcoming refugees by the thousands. My father was there. So my next bit of reasoning was that I would go to Hong Kong. I told this to Ah Paw, and her only reply was that I should return home and get the permission of my mother and brother.

Back in Siu Lo Chun I sat with my mother and brother and told them I wanted to go to Hong Kong where, I reminded them, my father was. My mother, Miu Hau, had no objection. In fact she said, "If you do not go to school you will become a farmer in the fields. Go." My brother asked me to give him a good reason for wanting to leave, and I told him of the new textbook that had been given out in our school which read, "We do not want our father. We do not want our mother. We only want New China." He agreed that I could go.

MY BROTHER, CHING MOH (LEFT), WITH A FRIEND AND MY COUSIN BUN YUEN (RIGHT), JUST MONTHS BEFORE MY BROTHER WAS KILLED IN 1952.

There was another occurrence at home that helped sway my brother. On that day when I spoke to my family, I was bitten on the face by a stray dog. My brother and his friends tracked down the dog, killed it and took some bile from its liver to treat the bite so there would be no infection. My brother thought this might be some omen and said, "Maybe you should go to Hong Kong."

"Yes, yes," I agreed, telling him I would continue to treat the dog bite with the bile.

I took two of my dresses, packed them into a square cloth, knotted, and walked back to Ah Paw's house, where I was given my usual space in her bedroom, which I then regarded as only temporary quarters. A cousin, who lived in Sah Gau, agreed to take me with her to Hong Kong three days later, and I spent most of my days running to my many friends in town telling them I was going to Hong Kong. Alone? they would ask, and when I said yes, they would call me brave. But I never felt brave.

In the evenings Ah Paw would talk to me. She told me she had confidence in me, that she had done her best to see to it that I was mature for my age, that I would speak up when I had to. Be strong, she said. When you want something, make sure you work hard to get it, no matter how hard the work is. "Things are not easy in the world," she cautioned. "You are a girl. Be careful with men. You are young now, but you are grow-ing up. Never drink, never. You never know what will happen when you drink."

She went on. "If people offer you money, and you have not done anything to earn it, never accept it. There is always a reason if someone gives you money. If you take it and spend it, you will have to do something for it. This will rob you of your in-dependence." As she spoke, she would, between pronouncements, look at me and kiss me on my forehead.

On the morning of the fourth day I left Ah Paw's house for the last time.

My cousin and I went by bus to Canton. There we got on a train, the Canton–Hong Kong Railway, which customarily went directly to Hong Kong. Not this time. The Kuomintang had bombed the tracks before they left. So we left the train at Lo Wu, changed to another and finally arrived in Hong Kong, where my father met me. He brought me to live with him in the home of my number-five aunt, Ng Ku Cheh, in Kowloon.

The front portion of my aunt's house was a small grocery, which my father helped tend. He was also a very good cook, had given me my very first rudimentary cooking lessons when he was home and he often cooked for my aunt and her family when they were busy in their shop. He was aware of my cooking efforts at my grand-mother's house, insisted that I help him, which I did, and in the nearly five months that we lived and worked under the same roof, he undertook to impart to me what-ever cooking knowledge he could.

Much of it was philosophical. He repeatedly said that it was as important to eat with one's eyes as it was with one's mouth. He placed great importance upon how a dish should appear when being presented. He stressed that when cooking, even if from a book, that I should keep an open mind and not simply and slavishly follow words alone. "Cook the way it has been written, but keep an open mind. If you keep walking only in a straight line, *nei wui jong doh chung*, you will go hard into a wall," he told me.

Follow the classical manner, he stressed, but warned that I not be a mindless im-itator. I listened.

Fried Rice with Sausages and Shrimp

(Lop Cheung Sin Har Chau Fan)

腊
腸
鮮
蝦
炒
飯

This fried rice is my father's variation on a theme. He did not use barbecued roast pork, nor did he use the sweet river shrimp that I remembered from my grandmother's kitchen. This *chau fan* relied upon the slight sweetness of the *lop cheung*, together with saltwater shrimp. Because these shrimp were dead, not live as the sweet river shrimp of Sah Gau had been, he taught me to make a marinade that would add flavor to the shrimp. I still consider this variation of fried rice my father's version, and I make it quite often in my kitchen.

MARINADE

½ teaspoon grated ginger mixed with 1 teaspoon Chinese white rice wine, or gin

½ teaspoon sugar

½ teaspoon sesame oil

1 teaspoon oyster sauce

½ teaspoon light soy sauce

Pinch white pepper

¼ pound shrimp, shelled, deveined, washed, dried and each cut in half lengthwise, then in half again

SAUCE

2 tablespoons oyster sauce

2 tablespoons Chicken Stock (page 13)

1 teaspoon light soy sauce

¼ teaspoon salt

½ teaspoon sesame oil

3½ tablespoons peanut oil

4 large eggs, beaten

1 teaspoon minced ginger

1 teaspoon minced garlic

4 Chinese sausages (*lop cheung*), cut into ⅓-inch dice

4 cups cooked rice

1 tablespoon coriander, finely sliced

3 scallions, finely sliced

Combine all ingredients for marinade. Add shrimp and allow to rest for 20 minutes. Reserve.

Mix all ingredients for sauce and reserve.

Heat wok over high heat for 45 seconds. Add 2 tablespoons peanut oil, coat wok with spatula. When a wisp of white smoke appears, add beaten eggs, scramble. Turn off heat and use spatula to break up eggs into small pieces. Set aside.

Wash wok and spatula. Heat wok over high heat 45 seconds. Add remaining peanut oil, coat wok with spatula. When a wisp of white smoke appears, add ginger and garlic and stir. When garlic turns light brown, add sausage, stir-fry for 3 minutes. Make a well in the center of the mixture, add shrimp and marinade, stir for 1 minute. Add cooked rice and stir together thoroughly 5 minutes until rice is very hot. Stir sauce, drizzle around rice. Mix well, until rice is coated. Add reserved eggs and mix together well. Add coriander and scallions, mix thoroughly. Remove to a heated plate and serve immediately.

SERVES 4

Lemon Rice Noodles

(Ling Mung Mai Fun)

In Hong Kong I found a wider use of cooking with citrus than I had experienced before. This dish of rice noodles, which I mixed with grated lemon skin (I didn't know the words *rind* or *zest* at the time) and lemon juice, was an invention encouraged by my father. It is fresh and different from a customary rice noodle dish.

3 tablespoons Scallion Oil (page 16)

1½ teaspoons minced garlic

½ teaspoon salt

1½ teaspoons grated lemon rind

½ cup Barbecued Pork (page 43), shredded

8 ounces rice noodles, fine, like angel hair, soaked in hot water 15–20 minutes until pliable, drained, loosened with chopsticks and cut into 4-inch lengths

1 tablespoon fresh lemon juice

4 teaspoons hot chili sauce (Tabasco preferred)

1½ teaspoons sesame oil

3 tablespoons scallions, finely sliced

Heat wok over high heat 45 seconds. Add scallion oil, coat wok with spatula, then add garlic and salt and stir. When garlic turns light brown, add lemon rind, stir. Add pork, stir for 30 seconds. Add noodles, lower heat and mix all ingredients together. Add lemon juice, toss. Add hot sauce, mix well. Add sesame oil, mix well again. When noodles are well coated, turn off heat. Add scallions, mix well, transfer to a heated platter and serve immediately.

SERVES 4

Boiled Noodles in Sesame Sauce

(Mah Jeung Lo Mein)

This noodle dish from Ah Paw's kitchen was a surprise for my father, who after tasting it actually asked me how I made it.

SAUCE

3 tablespoons sesame seed paste diluted with 3 tablespoons boiling Vegetable Stock (page 14)

2½ tablespoons Scallion Oil (page 16)

1 tablespoon dark soy sauce

1 tablespoon light soy sauce

3 tablespoons oyster sauce

1½ teaspoons Chinese white rice vinegar, or distilled white vinegar

1 tablespoon sesame oil

1½ teaspoons minced garlic

2 teaspoons minced ginger

1 tablespoon sugar

¼ teaspoon salt

Pinch white pepper

3 tablespoons scallions, finely sliced

10 cups cold water

2 teaspoons salt

12 ounces fine (similar to capellini) fresh egg noodles

In a large bowl, place all sauce ingredients, mix thoroughly and reserve.

In a large pot place water and salt, bring to a boil over high heat. Add noodles, cook for 1½ minutes until al dente, stirring and loosening as they cook with chopsticks or fork. Turn off heat, drain noodles well. Then add directly into the bowl of sauce, mix well to coat the noodles thoroughly. Serve warm, in the bowl.

SERVES 4

IN MAY OF 1950 MY MOTHER, Miu Hau, traveled from Siu Lo Chun to Hong Kong, at the urging of my brother, in an effort to persuade my father and me to return home. It was a determined effort on her part, for in those times of mass exodus, while it was relatively easy to leave China, it was more difficult, though not impossible, to return. My mother was permitted to leave when she explained that she was trying to bring her husband and daughter back to China. As it turned out, she was successful with my father, but not with me. I had made up my mind and I would not change it, I told my mother, adding that perhaps in the future I would return to my home for a visit.

MY BROTHER CHING MOH, IN HIS PEOPLE'S REPUBLIC OF CHINA MILITARY UNIFORM IN 1951.

During the first two of the four years I lived with Aunt Number Five behind her store in Kowloon, my brother wrote to me many times asking me to return home. I continued to say no. I remember that in 1952, his letters stopped. I was informed by a cousin through his family in Siu Lo Chun that my brother had been arrested. Shortly after, a letter from my father arrived, telling me Ching Moh had been executed by party authorities in our village. He had been accused, falsely it turned out, of being a Kuomintang agent. The charge was not true, but my brother was dead.

Did I feel sorrow that I had not returned home? Yes, but I did not cry in front of my aunt, remembering that Ah Paw had told me never to cry where it could be seen, but to breathe heavily, to bite my lips, but never cry. I did however run to the bathroom and cry there. I also realized that my being home might not have made a difference. I know I would have supported my brother, and perhaps I might have been killed as well. When I stopped crying I swore that I would never again return to my village, the village that had killed my brother. In all of my visits to China since, I have kept to this promise. I have never returned to Siu Lo Chun.

At this time I was going to an evening school to learn English. A friend and customer of my aunt, a Mr. Ng, asked me one day if I was attending school. I told him I was not because I could not afford it. He said immediately, "You are now in my school." So I worked in the shop days and took evening English classes. This was a happy time that was interrupted by another shock when, in 1954, a letter from one of my cousins in Sah Gau informed me that Ah Paw had died.

I did cry then, and for a long time. Biting my lips did not help. I was so surprised. She had never been ill in all the time I was with her. I supposed I thought she would live forever. I always thought I would one day return to see her, because I never thought of her as old. As it turned out, she was about seventy-two when she passed away, from what my cousin called old age. The other news from Sah Gau was equally

WITH MY COUSIN MAUREEN IN 1954, IN FAN LING IN HONG KONG'S NEW
TERRITORIES, WHERE FOR A TIME I LIVED, WORKED AND LEARNED ENGLISH.

saddening. My cousin Ah Mui, Ah Paw's grandson, with whom I had trapped shrimp
for Ah Paw's mynah, was now, along with his wife, a member of the Communist Party.
In fact Ah Mui had been appointed a provincial official, and transferred north to
Guangzhi. Because of his position, most of Ah Paw's small empire remained intact, but
the servants had left, Ah Guk to her family nearby, Sao Lin to Siu Lo Chun to care for
my mother, who was ill.

I left Kowloon for my first job, that of a salesgirl in a shop called Nina Silk Store.
It was in the New Territories town of Fan Ling, where I lived with my cousin Maureen.
My evening school classes ended, but I was proud that I had gotten my first job.
Though I earned very little money, HK$100, the equivalent of about US$25 each
month, I regularly sent some of it back to my parents.

They had no income. Their lands had been confiscated. All they had was their
house, one wall of which had collapsed, I was informed by letter. What had been a
pleasant flower garden was overgrown. Our fish ponds were no longer ours. No longer
were our fields ours. There was little food in our market, and inflation was rampant. I
needed to support them as much as I could.

IN A PUBLIC GARDEN IN FAN LING IN 1955.
THIS GARDEN HAS BEEN REPLACED WITH
A FORTY-STORY APARTMENT BUILDING.

I remember when I went to work the first day, the owner, a man from India, gave me that one day to memorize and place his entire stock. I did it. It was like going to school all over again.

I thought always of my family and my Ah Paw in those days, never more so than one day when another shop owner, a Pakistani, gave me an envelope with HK$100 inside, which represented my salary for one month. I recalled Ah Paw's cautions about never taking money I had not earned, so I declined his gift. As it turned out, he was on the lookout for a young wife and he thought I would do just fine. I thought not, and I silently thanked Ah Paw again.

I stayed in Fan Ling for two years, then moved back to Hong Kong proper, to Kowloon, to another home and another job. My number-six aunt, Lok Ku Cheh, Maureen's mother, took me into her home, which I shared with her and four cousins, three teenage girls and a boy. It was my happiest time in Hong Kong. I worked, then managed, a fabrics and tailor shop, Hira Silk Store, in the mall-like Chung King Arcade off Nathan Road. In addition to having a job with more responsibilities, which I liked, I

IN 1957 BEHIND THE COUNTER OF THE HIRA SILK STORE ON NATHAN ROAD IN KOWLOON, WHICH I MANAGED FOR THREE YEARS.

had a schedule that gave me every second Sunday afternoon off, no easy accomplishment in Hong Kong where just about everybody worked morning until night, seven days each week, with time off only on major holidays.

Lok Ku Cheh was another of my extended family who was a fine cook, and I learned much from her. In my time off I watched her, cooked with her and learned. I amazed her when I showed her how expertly I could kill a chicken, and when she asked me how I knew, I told her I had learned in Ah Paw's kitchen. She understood.

MY GRANDMOTHER'S CHINESE KITCHEN

Even though she was from my father's side of our family, and Ah Paw had been the matriarch of my mother's side, the reputation of my grandmother's kitchen was well known, she said. She also welcomed my occasional help in her kitchen and admired my love for cooking because, she said, none of her own daughters seemed interested in it. It was from Lok Ku Cheh that I learned what has become a true kitchen heirloom of my family.

SHORTLY AFTER THIS PICTURE WAS TAKEN, I MOVED TO KOWLOON AND THE HOME OF MY NUMBER-SIX AUNT, LOK KU CHEH.

My Aunt's Lemon Chicken

(Ling Mung Gai)

This recipe, from Lok Ku Cheh, my father's younger sister, is unique. There are many preparations that go by the name of Lemon Chicken, but virtually all of them involve deep-frying big pieces of chicken breast that have been dipped in batter, then doused with a viscous, usually overly-sweet lemon sauce. Lok Ku Cheh's lemon chicken is a dish of great harmony, lively and natural, that consists of an entire fresh chicken, cut up, and steamed with fresh lemons. Lok Ku Cheh always specified that a young chicken be used for this dish, a *chee gai*, or virgin chicken that had never laid eggs, because its bones were soft and delightful on which to chew. These days, a three-pound chicken is the best approximation to use. I recommend, and cook, this dish quite often, and I teach it repeatedly.

1 3-pound chicken, fat and membranes removed, rubbed with ¼ cup salt, rinsed under cold water, drained, dried with paper towels and cut into bite-size pieces

1 fresh lemon, cut into 4 quarters

MARINADE

2 teaspoons Chinese white rice wine, or gin mixed with ¾ teaspoon ginger juice

1 tablespoon light soy sauce

1½ tablespoons oyster sauce

1½ teaspoons sesame oil

2 tablespoons peanut oil

1½ teaspoons salt

1 tablespoon sugar

Pinch white pepper

2½ tablespoons cornstarch

1 tablespoon scallions, finely sliced

1 tablespoon coriander, finely sliced

Place chicken pieces in a bowl, squeeze lemon quarters over them, then add quarters to the bowl. Add all marinade ingredients, mix to combine well. Allow to rest 30 minutes.

Place chicken in a steamproof dish, spread pieces out and pour marinade over them. Place dish in a steamer, over 8 cups boiling water, cover and steam, 40 to 50 minutes. Turn chicken 2 to 3 times during steaming (see steaming directions, page 30). The chicken is cooked when it turns white. Turn off heat and remove from steamer. Serve chicken in its steamproof dish, sprinkled with sliced scallions and coriander, with cooked rice.

SERVES 4 TO 6

Chicken Pancakes

(Gai Yuk Bang)

This very unusual dish, from Ah Paw's kitchen, became a family favorite as well. It has always been an inherited dish, from my grandmother, to me, to my aunt, soon to my granddaughter. I have never seen it in a restaurant. Lok Ku Cheh had never heard of it, but when I described it as it has been made in Sah Gau, she took to it immediately, one reason being that it fit into her lifestyle, for she cooked every day for at least six people.

1 pound ground chicken

4 scallions, finely sliced

⅓ cup water chestnuts, cut into ¼-inch dice

3 tablespoons egg white, lightly beaten

2 teaspoons Chinese white rice wine, or gin mixed with 1 teaspoon ginger juice

2 teaspoons sesame oil

2 tablespoons peanut oil

1½ tablespoons oyster sauce

2 teaspoons light soy sauce

¼ teaspoon salt

2 teaspoons sugar

Pinch white pepper

1½ tablespoons cornstarch

7 tablespoons peanut oil, for pan-frying

Mix all ingredients, except 7 tablespoons peanut oil, until thoroughly blended. Divide mixture into 2 equal portions.

Heat wok over high heat 40 seconds. Add 2 tablespoons peanut oil, coat wok with spatula. When a wisp of white smoke appears, add one portion of chicken mixture and with spatula flatten the mixture to make a pancake about 6½ inches in diameter. Lower heat, tip wok side to side to ensure even browning. Add 1 additional tablespoon of peanut oil if needed. If so, drizzle into the wok from its edges. Fry for 4 minutes. Turn over, fry another 4 minutes, again tipping wok back and forth. Again, if chicken mixture is too dry, drizzle another tablespoon of peanut oil into the wok.

Repeat with second half of chicken mixture. After each pancake is golden brown, remove to a heated dish. When both are cooked, serve with cooked rice.

SERVES 4

NOTE You may make this into 4 pancakes, by dividing mixture into 4 equal portions. Cook in same manner.

These pancakes were as versatile as they were popular. We ate them alone, with rice, as noted, but we also cut them up to be added to soups or eaten with noodles, and stir-fried them with vegetables.

Chicken Pancakes Stir-Fried with Long Beans

(DAU GAW CHAU GAI YUK BANG)

Long beans are a distinctly Asian vegetable. They resemble string beans, but often grow more than two feet long. Their name, *dau gaw*, translates as "bean horns." In my grandmother's garden both green and white long beans grew. Those green were generally more crisp and were used in stir-fries; the white were used in long-cooked methods such as braising, where they softened. Their tastes were similar. Long beans are available in Asian markets. If unavailable, use string beans.

SAUCE

3 tablespoons oyster sauce

2 teaspoons double dark soy sauce

1 teaspoon sesame oil

2 teaspoons sugar

Pinch white pepper

3 tablespoons peanut oil

1 tablespoon minced ginger

½ teaspoon salt

½ cup scallions, white portions only, cut into ½-inch pieces on the diagonal

1 pound long beans, washed, dried, both ends trimmed and each cut into 2-inch lengths

1½ tablespoons Shao-Hsing wine, or sherry

1 Chicken Pancake (page 218), 8 ounces, cooked, cut into slices 2 inches long by ½ inch wide

Mix sauce ingredients, reserve.

Heat wok over high heat 40 seconds, add peanut oil, coat wok with spatula. When a wisp of white smoke appears add ginger and stir. Add salt and stir. Add scallions, stir and mix, cook 45 seconds. Add long beans, stir-fry 1½ minutes. Drizzle wine into wok along its edges, mix well. Cook for 1 minute. Stir sauce, make a well in mixture, pour sauce in. Mix well to coat the beans, allow to cook 5 to 7 minutes. Little or no liquid should be in wok at this point.

Add chicken pancake slices, stir to mix well. Cook 2 minutes, until hot. There will be virtually no liquid in the wok at this point. Turn off heat, transfer to a heated dish and serve with cooked rice.

SERVES 4 TO 6

WITH FRED IN 1959, AS WE SAT ON THE STAR FERRY
CROSSING HONG KONG HARBOR.

FROM MY NUMBER-SIX AUNT'S HOUSE, Hong Kong's many small street markets were just short walks away and the produce available was remarkable: vegetables just in from the New Territory farms, live chickens, ducks and squabs, live fish, shrimp and shellfish. I recall my aunt going off to her market, the Chung Choi Gai, with pail in hand, to buy that evening's live fish. These days many of these small markets have been replaced by large, consolidated covered markets and sprawling outdoor enclaves in Sham Sui Po and Yau Mah Tei.

Lok Ku Cheh was a kind woman who, even though she had six children of her own, gave her love to me. She counseled me, as my mother would have had she been there, and as my Ah Paw when she was alive. And when I met the man who would eventually become my husband, it was Lok Ku Cheh who took me in hand and planned an elaborate lunch for him that was in fact a let-us-look-at-this-foreign-devil invitation, but which Fred believed to be a welcome-to-the-family meal.

I remember that day as one in which I did most of the late cooking, while my aunt, who had cooked all morning, sat smoking with Fred. He smoked quite a bit then, and my aunt did likewise. He spoke no Chinese, she spoke no English, but as I cooked in

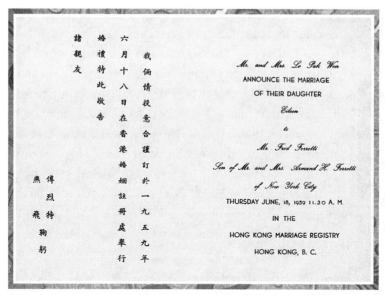

諸親友

婚禮特此敬告

六月十八日在香港婚姻註冊處舉行

我倆情投意合謹訂於一九五九年

燕傳烈飛特鞠躬

Mr. and Mrs. Lo Pak Wen
ANNOUNCE THE MARRIAGE
OF THEIR DAUGHTER
Eileen
to
Mr. Fred Ferretti
Son of Mr. and Mrs. Armand H. Ferretti
of New York City
THURSDAY JUNE, 18, 1959 11.30 A. M.
IN THE
HONG KONG MARRIAGE REGISTRY
HONG KONG, B. C.

OUR WEDDING ANNOUNCEMENT.

her kitchen I heard them laughing uproariously at, and with, each other. Then the food began to come in. Fred was quite proud of the way he held chopsticks. He had been drafted into the U.S. Army, was stationed in Japan and had learned to use chopsticks. My aunt, however, was unimpressed. She watched him eat for a short while then said to me, *"Koi tung yap boon jai sik fan yat yeung."* Fred asked what she had said. I told him, that Lok Ku Cheh had said, "You eat like a Japanese," and that it wasn't a compliment.

To close the meal, my aunt brought in a very large flat garoupa, a fish of the Hong Kong waters. She had steamed it and it lay, as Fred likes to tell the story, with a large cooked eye staring at him. I should add that at this point in his life, Fred's only experience with fish had been canned tuna. He asked me, in a whisper, "What do I do?" I responded, "Take some fish."

Very tentatively he pushed his chopsticks into the fish, took some bits and placed it atop his bowl of rice. My aunt would have none of that. She said loudly, *"M'ho gum hak hei,"* or "Don't be bashful," grabbed his bowl and with her chopsticks, pushed fish onto the rice, including that eye. "What do I do now?" he asked. "Eat it," I replied.

What he did was put his glass of beer close to his left hand then, with the same hand, he lifted his rice bowl to his lips, and with his right hand shoveled the fish, and its eye, into his mouth, barely chewing, swallowing loudly, then finishing up with a

huge gulp of beer. My aunt thought this was hilarious, and never ceased telling her family of Fred's small adventure.

I had met my future husband a year earlier when he happened to come into the shop that I managed. He introduced himself, asked my name, said he was on leave from his station in Japan and wished to have a shirt tailored. I suppose he liked his shirt, for he had another made, then a jacket. He came to the shop every day. Then, perhaps after the fifth visit, he asked if I would go out with him. I refused. He followed me home on my bus one night, we shared coffees in a teahouse, and he shocked me by saying that he intended to marry me. My cousins seemed to like him, and eventually we did have a date; a chaperoned lunch, a couple of days before Lok Ku Cheh's lunch.

He left Hong Kong, and we corresponded for slightly less than a year. Then he returned and in a flurry of activity we were licensed to be married, then married. I had my visa approved and issued in one day. We were both given visas for Japan, where we had a brief honeymoon, then we flew on to the United States, all in ten days. It was Aunt Number Six who became my surrogate mother in that year, from the time Fred and I met, until we left Hong Kong. It was Lok Ku Cheh, with my four cousins, who planned and arranged our wedding reception, which by the way, was held before we were married simply because we had to schedule it on a day when most people would be off from work. It was fine. It was fun. I left Hong Kong nine years after I had arrived there from Ah Paw's house.

NINE

TO MY KITCHEN

進入我廚房

THE LESSONS I HAD LEARNED IN my grandmother's kitchen were put to the severest of tests very shortly after my arrival in the United States. What was accepted here as Chinese food, was not. What was widely regarded as authentic Chinese cooking, was not. All manner of so-called Chinese foods were to be found in cans and packages, and in the frozen compartments of markets. I quickly became quite homesick for the food I had cooked and eaten in my home and that of my grandmother.

My disorientation began with a dinner my new parents-in-law gave in my honor at their favorite local Chinese restaurant. As they ordered, out came *chau mein*, not a beautiful tangle of fresh noodles with vegetables and perhaps some pork, but a solid soft mass of cornstarched cabbage, celery and onions sitting on fried, but soggy noodles; and egg fu yung, not the fluffy, light scramble of eggs with tiny shrimp it was supposed to be, but a Frisbee-like disk covered with a thick brown sauce. I called the manager and asked him, in Chinese, *"Nei yau moh chung guok choi?"* which translated literally means, "Do you have any food from China?"

He smiled at me. I told him I had just come from Hong Kong two days earlier, and I could not eat this food. He asked what could he cook for me. I asked him if he had any barbecued pork. He said yes. I asked if he had any *choi sum* (lettuce). He said yes. Well then, I asked, could you stir-fry some of both together for me, and give me a bowl of cooked rice. Which he did, and I enjoyed my meal. My new parents liked the dish as well, even though they thought it odd.

Only a few days later, I recall that my husband, to surprise and please me, stopped off at a market on the way home from work and walked in with a package of frozen sweet and sour pork, a can of fried noodles and a can of bean sprouts for me. His heart was surely in the right place, but when I opened the cans, defrosted and heated the pork, I simply could not eat even a bite. At that point I said the next time he thought of shopping for me, it should be to take me to New York City's Chinatown.

He did, and I bought not only a collection of woks, cleavers, steamers, ladles, spatulas, strainers and brushes, but rice, peanut oil and sesame oil, soy and oyster sauces, and an assortment of dried foods, to set up my first Chinese kitchen in America.

All of these were available, but the more unfamiliar of Chinese foodstuffs that had been commonplace to me growing up, were not always available. The American supermarket was of little help. Meats and chickens were in parts, frozen, or sitting on ice. There were no vegetables that I could call truly Chinese, but there were watercress, lettuce, spinach, cabbage, broccoli, cauliflower, carrots, celery and string beans of middling quality, though not of the crisp versions of those I remembered from my grandmother's walled garden. There was no ginger, and garlic, when available, came two small purple bulbs to a box. Most soy sauces were thin and salt-laden. I remember buying a bottle, opening it, tasting it and resolving never to cook with it.

In general, the vegetables displayed in Chinatown shops—vegetables grown on New Jersey truck farms for the expanding enclave of Chinese immigrants in lower Manhattan—were better. I found live chickens and fish, which pleased me, but the water chestnuts were only in cans. It was a mixed, if recognizable, bag. I thought of my father's dictum, that one should learn to turn corners or one would walk into walls, and I began cooking Chinese food. My shopping forays into Chinatown came at least twice a week.

It should be noted that at this time, Chinatown was itself somewhat insular. Quite often, as I walked its streets with my non-Chinese husband, unpleasantries

IN FRONT OF MY WALL OF WOKS AT HOME.

were growled at me. Not only did I ignore them, but I did not explain them to my husband.

Soon I became used to Chinatown. I found small shops with some of the essentials I had been used to. I found fresh noodles and bean curd factories, and I found Mr. Leung. My Leung was a middle-aged man, whose family had come from a part of China reasonably close to where I had been born. He was a kind man, who tended his food shop always wearing knee-high boots, and a thick denim apron.

He greeted me pleasantly. He listened as I talked about my wishes to outfit a proper Chinese kitchen, and even as we talked, he cut off a small piece from the juicy middle of a length of barbecued pork and gave it to my little son, Christopher. My relationship with Mr. Leung became long and fruitful. He was the first Chinese friend I made in America.

Over the years this once-small plot of downtown Manhattan has become big and sprawling, in virtually every way, a Chinese city within the ultimate American city. The quality of foods offered and sold can be exceptional. It is my market, and I take friends, Western chefs and students there by the dozens to introduce them to the true tastes of my food. I consider my food part of my heritage, for that is what Ah Paw taught me, and it is what I preach. Fine Chinese cooking is as it was in my grandmother's kitchen in Sah Gau, of fresh ingredients presented unadorned, with essential flavors unmasked by heavy sauces, with poultry and meats, fish and seafoods, cooked so that their tastes are true.

In my kitchen I have taught my children that food is a part of their shared culture, that it is tradition and custom, as well as nourishment. I know they believe it. And, in what has now become my own grandmother's kitchen, I have begun imparting that which I was taught, what was instilled in my bones, to my granddaughter. As early as the age of one, she would watch, unmoving, her eyes wide with interest, as I stirred, mixed, boiled and otherwise cooked food on my stove for her. She ate chicken that had been poached in stock, yams, potatoes, broccoli and carrots, cut finely for her. My husband would hold her for long periods simply because she wanted to watch what was a mystery. But soon it won't be.

My kitchen grew as I acquired space. Two apartment kitchens were confining, to be sure, but once our family moved into a large home my kitchen swelled to include some cabinetry reworking to accommodate a large gas-fired professional stove and oven, a collection of more than thirty woks, carbon steel and iron for stir-frying, stainless steel for steaming, even aluminum, as a brief experiment. Most of them are traditional round-bottom woks, the best, and a couple of flat-bottoms that I use when I must do demonstration classes on portable electric ranges. I have acquired more than twenty traditional woven bamboo steamers, also the best.

One technique I have developed in my kitchen is tempering. The clay and ceramic dishes of China seemed never to crack in the heat of steam, but I found that some in the West do. Tempering (see page 230) will ensure that your porcelains and Pyrexes will not crack when heated.

I acquired a whole herd of cleavers of various sizes and weights, to cut, slice and mince, to chop, to cut fish, to slice vegetables. And I have collected as well big round steel strainers and wire strainers, from as small as three inches across to fourteen inches in diameter.

All of these are the bedrock of my kitchen, in which I have taught private classes, before becoming a teaching chef at the China Institute, and the New School in New York City. Without the limitations of space, I have been able to expand upon what I learned as a girl, even to go beyond that teaching. In China, for example, we virtually never made dim sum dumplings, those little dots on the heart so beloved in southern China. They are time-consuming to make, and in China, the teahouses and dim sum parlors were accessible. But why should I not make them? I believed that there surely would be an audience, even if only among those who loved the experience of working with flours and those doughs that come alive in one's hands.

MY SON STEVEN, AGE FIVE, IN 1974.

IN A CLASS FOR IMMIGRANTS AT THE CHINA INSTITUTE IN 1979, IN WHICH THEY WERE TAUGHT BASIC ENGLISH, COOKING TECHNIQUES, AND RESTAURANT SERVICE. WE WERE VISITED BY SEVERAL CHEFS FROM THE PEOPLE'S REPUBLIC OF CHINA, THE FIRST SUCH PROFESSIONAL VISIT.

TEMPERING

Porcelain dishes and Pyrexes may be used inside of steamers, but first they must be seasoned or tempered. Fill a wok with five to six cups cold water, place a rack in the wok and stack the dishes to be tempered on the rack, making certain they are completely covered with cold water. Cover wok, bring water to a boil, allow to boil 10 minutes. Turn off heat, allow wok to cool to room temperature. The dishes are now seasoned, permanently, and can be placed in steamers without fearing they will crack. It has been suggested that Pyrex is already tempered, but this applies only for Pyrex dishes that will go into an oven.

Dough for Steamed Buns

(BAU MIN TEUN)

This dough, which uses bleached flour as a base, is ideal for buns with fillings ranging from chicken, to vegetables, to red bean and lotus seed pastes. Unfilled, this dough steams into soft, spongelike, slightly sweet breads often eaten with fried poultry.

As many of us know, flours react differently based upon seasons, climate and the presence or lack of moisture. By a process of many trials I have found one flour to be the best for this dough in the United States: Gold Medal All-Purpose Enriched Bleached Flour. I specify bleached because the Chinese admire its snowy whiteness as much as they do the whiteness of cooked rice. The use of lard is an old tradition. Use it if you wish.

2¼ cups flour

3½ teaspoons baking powder

½ cup sugar

3 ounces milk

1½ ounces water

3 tablespoons lard at room temperature, or peanut oil

Mix flour, baking powder and sugar together on a work surface. Make a well in the center of the mixture. Add milk gradually, working it with the fingers. Once milk has been absorbed, add water and continue to work the mix into a dough. Add lard, or peanut oil, and again, continue to work down with the fingers.

Using a dough scraper, gather dough in one hand and begin kneading with the other. Knead for 12 to 15 minutes. If dough is dry, add 1 teaspoon of water at a time and continue to knead, until the dough becomes elastic. If dough is wet, sprinkle a bit of flour on the work surface and on your hands and continue kneading.

When dough is elastic, cover with a damp cloth and allow to rest for about 1 hour. The dough is now ready for use.

Steamed Pork Buns

(Jing Char Siu Bau)

These particular steamed buns were favorites of my grandmother, who would send her servants off to the teahouse to buy them, then re-steam them in her kitchen. I recall that every month, on the day after her observance of her self-imposed Buddhist day of vegetarianism in mid-month, Ah Paw would enjoy these pork-filled buns. No one in my family enjoys them more than my daughter, Elena. One year when she came home from college with a classmate, the two of them ate fourteen of them! I hope her daughter, my granddaughter, Siu Siu, loves them as much.

SAUCE

1½ tablespoons oyster sauce

1½ teaspoons dark soy sauce

1 tablespoon ketchup

2¼ teaspoons sugar

Pinch white pepper

1 tablespoon tapioca starch

2½ ounces Chicken Stock (page 14)

1½ tablespoons peanut oil

½ cup onions, cut into ¼-inch dice

¾ cup Barbecued Pork (page 43), sliced paper thin, into squares ⅓ inch on a side

1½ teaspoons Chinese white rice wine, or gin

½ teaspoon sesame oil

1 recipe Dough for Steamed Buns (page 231)

16 squares of waxed paper 2½ inches on a side

2 tablespoons Scallion Oil (page 16)

Mix all ingredients for sauce; reserve.

MAKE THE PORK BUN FILLING: Heat wok over high heat 40 seconds. Add peanut oil, coat wok with spatula. When a wisp of white smoke appears, add onions, lower heat, cook, turning occasionally until onions turn light brown, about 4 minutes. Add pork, raise heat, stir-fry with onions for 2 minutes. Add wine, mix well. Lower heat, stir sauce, pour in, stir until mixture thickens and turns brown, 2 to 3 minutes. Add sesame oil, mix well. Turn off heat. Remove pork filling and transfer to a shallow dish. Allow to cool to room temperature. Refrigerate, uncovered, 4 hours, or covered, overnight.

PREPARE THE BUNS: Roll steamed bun dough into a cylinder 16 inches long. Cut into 1-inch pieces. Roll each piece into a ball. Work with one piece at a time, cover those not being used with damp cloth.

Press ball of dough down lightly, then, working with the fingers of both hands, press dough into a dome-like well shape. Place 1 tablespoon of filling in center of well. Close and pleat dough with fingers until filling is completely enclosed. Twist and pinch off last bits of dough. Repeat until 16 buns are formed. (Use only 1 tablespoon of filling at the outset, until you have learned to work well with the dough. Otherwise you may have trouble sealing the buns. When you are more comfortable, increase amount of filling to 1½ to 2 tablespoons.)

Place buns on squares of waxed paper, sealed sides up. Place in steamer 2 inches apart to allow for expansion. Steam for 15 to 20 minutes (page 30). The buns are done when they are snowy white, and their tops, where they were sealed, will open like a flower, revealing a bit of the filling. Brush bun with scallion oil and serve.

MAKES 16 BUNS

NOTE These buns will keep 3 to 4 days after steaming, refrigerated. To reheat, steam for 5 minutes. They may also be frozen, after steaming, and will keep 2 to 3 months. To reheat, defrost thoroughly, steam for 5 minutes until very hot.

Steamed Sausage Buns

(Lop Cheung Guen)

腊
腸
卷

When I was young, these steamed sausage buns were a winter treat, because the pork sausages were made only in the cold months. The impatience of waiting, the expectation, made them even more of a seasonal treat. When I found that *lop cheung* was readily available in Asian markets, at any time, I quickly made these remembrances from my childhood.

3 tablespoons oyster sauce

3 tablespoons dark soy sauce

1 tablespoon sesame oil

8 Chinese pork sausages (*lop cheung*), each cut in half on the diagonal

1 recipe Dough for Steamed Buns (page 231)

16 pieces of waxed paper, cut into 3½-inches by 2-inches pieces

2 tablespoons Scallion Oil (page 16)

In a shallow dish combine oyster sauce, soy sauce and sesame oil. Add sausage pieces and marinate for 30 minutes.

MAKE THE BUNS: Roll Steamed Bun Dough into a cylinder 16 inches long. Cut into 1-inch pieces. Work with 1 piece at a time, covering those remaining with a damp cloth. Roll each piece into a sausage shape 12 inches long. Press sausage piece by its thinly cut end together with one end of the dough length. Then press and wrap dough in a spiral around the sausage length. When the end is reached, press it into the sausage to seal. Both ends of the sausage will be visible at the ends of the dough spiral.

Place each sausage roll on a piece of waxed paper. Place in steamer, 1 inch apart, to allow for expansion. Steam 15 to 20 minutes, until snowy white. (See steaming directions, page 30.) Remove from steamer, brush with scallion oil and serve immediately.

MAKES 16 ROLLS

NOTE These buns will keep, after steaming, 3 to 4 days, refrigerated. To reheat, steam 5 minutes. They may be frozen, after steaming, and will keep 2 to 3 months. To reheat, allow to defrost and steam 5 minutes, until very hot.

THERE WERE SEVERAL MISADVENTURES ALONG THE way as I developed my own kitchen. I found, when I was pregnant with my first son, Christopher, that the aromas of Chinese cooking with which I was most familiar tended to make me nauseous. What to do? I cooked with several bottles of air freshener in the kitchen. Then, after my son's birth I knew I had to make my sweet birth vinegar. It took several days to get a sufficient amount of black vinegar from Chinatown, and several visits to the butcher to get enough pigs' feet. But I made it, virtually redecorating a kitchen wall in the process.

Repeatedly, I was unable to buy wine, or spirits, even beer, because I looked too young. I recall going into a liquor shop to buy a bottle of white wine to use for cooking, and I was asked for identification. I told the clerk that I did not even have my green card with me. He refused. Another time, after my daughter was born I went to buy some beer, wheeling her into the store in a stroller. I told the clerk that she was my daughter, which he did not believe, and I was unable to buy beer.

My husband thought all of this was hilarious, until he became part of my travail. I was teaching a class in Peking Duck, and it is my custom that each student receive a duck and prepare it from scratch. My bonus is always that I keep the livers and make pate of them. Well, on this occasion I found that I had no red wine to add to the livers. I telephoned my husband and he said that he was busy and to just take the best. Which one, I asked. Take a very good wine, he said, because a good pate needs a good wine. When he came home that evening and saw that I had opened, and used completely, a 1982 Chateau Lynch-Bages, he wanted to know why. I told him I had followed his advice and opened a good one.

"But that was very good," he said.

"How was the pate?" I asked.

"Wonderful," he replied.

I smiled and turned away. Never again was there any question about driving to Chinatown, where my age was never in question, to buy wine and spirits to drink, or to cook with.

I continued to fashion and to cook the many dim sum that I knew from my past. Those available in Chinatown teahouses were passable, but not always up to the standard I remembered. I learned early to make *woo gok*, which consist of mashed taro root folded around savory fillings, because these had been my husband's discovery in Hong Kong. I made *har gau*, those pleated shrimp dumplings, and spring rolls, as well as *lor bok goh*, turnip cake, and *sang maw mah tai goh*, water chestnut cake, just as I had made them in Ah Paw's New Year kitchen. Two of my earliest successes were with other dim sum traditions.

Water Dumplings

(Soi Gau)

These are among the simpler dim sum to make, and quite attractive as well. As with many other dim sum, they can be fashioned from ready-made skins or wrappings, in this instance won ton skins. Though they are called "water dumplings," they are actually boiled in water, then heated in stock and served in the resulting soup.

FILLING

12 ounces shrimp, washed, shelled, deveined, dried and cut into quarters then chopped into a paste

12 ounces ground pork

1½ teaspoons salt

1 teaspoon grated ginger mixed with 1 teaspoon Chinese white rice wine, or gin

⅓ cup bamboo shoots, cut into ¼-inch dice

2½ teaspoons sugar

1½ teaspoons sesame oil

1 tablespoon peanut oil

1½ teaspoons light soy sauce

2 tablespoons oyster sauce

3 tablespoons cornstarch

Pinch white pepper

40 won ton skins, each cut with a kitchen shears into a circle 2¾ inches in diameter

3 quarts water

5 cups Chicken Stock (page 13)

1 cup chives, cut into ¼-inch lengths

Combine filling ingredients in a large bowl, mix well to combine thoroughly. Refrigerate 4 hours uncovered, or overnight, covered.

MAKE THE DUMPLINGS: Work with the trimmed won ton skins, keeping a small bowl of water at hand. Place 1 tablespoon of filling in the center of the skin. With a butter knife, brush water around the edges of the skin. Fold skin into a half-moon shape, press edges together with thumb and forefinger to seal. Place completed dumpling on a cornstarch-dusted cookie sheet. Repeat until all dumplings are made. As you work, keep reserved skins under a damp cloth to prevent drying out.

In a pot bring 3 quarts of water to a boil. Add dumplings and boil 5 to 7 minutes, until filling can be seen through skin. Run cold water over dumplings in the pot to stop the cooking process, then drain.

In a pot bring chicken stock to a boil, add chives and stir. Add dumplings, stir. Return to a boil, turn off heat and serve immediately.

MAKES 40 WATER DUMPLINGS

A BOWL OF FINISHED WATER
DUMPLINGS FROM A COOKING
CLASS IN MY HOME.

Cook-and-Sell Dumplings

(Siu Mai)

These dumplings are widely known by their Chinese name rather than by its translation. Their name, *siu mai*, usually pronounced quickly, means "cook and sell," and is meant to indicate that these little basket-shaped dim sum are so good that they are eaten immediately upon serving, and not one is ever left unsold. Like the water dumpling recipes above, these dumplings are fashioned from won ton skins.

FILLING

8 Chinese black mushrooms, soaked 15–20 minutes in hot water until softened, washed, squeezed, dried, stems discarded and caps cut into ¼-inch dice

½ pound pork, coarsely ground

¼ pound shrimp, shelled, deveined, washed and cut into ¼-inch dice

½ teaspoon salt

1½ teaspoons sugar

1 teaspoon peanut oil

1 tablespoon oyster sauce

1 tablespoon cornstarch

1 teaspoon sesame oil

Pinch white pepper

20 won ton skins, cut with kitchen shears into circles 2¼ inches in diameter

Sufficient lettuce leaves to line steamer, trimmed

In a large bowl, combine all filling ingredients. Mix, stirring in one direction, until consistency is smooth and even. Place in shallow dish, refrigerate 4 hours, uncovered, or overnight, covered.

MAKE DUMPLINGS: Holding a round dumpling skin in one hand, place 4 teaspoons of filling in center and pat down to flatten. With your fingers fold up the skin while turning the dumpling and flattening the filling on top with a rounded butter knife. Continue turning and flattening until a basket-shape is formed. The diameter will be about 1¼ inches.

Pack down, and smooth the top of the filling. Squeeze the dumpling lightly to create a "neck." This helps to keep the dumpling intact during steaming. Tap dumpling lightly on work surface to flatten the bottom so that it will stand upright in steamer. Place layer of lettuce leaves in steamer. Place dumplings on leaves, allowing at least ½ inch between dumplings.

Place 10 cups boiling water in wok. Put in steamer, cover, steam 7 to 9 minutes, until pork is off-white and firm. (See steaming directions, page 30.) Serve immediately.

N O T E Won ton skins come in 1-pound packages, usually 60 to 80 skins per pound, depending upon their thickness. Any remaining unused skins may be frozen for future use. The *siu mai* may be frozen as well, after steaming. They will keep 2 to 3 months, wrapped first in plastic, then in foil. To reheat, defrost and steam 3 to 5 minutes.

A JOURNEY COMES FULL CIRCLE

The more I cooked, the more my sense of what I was doing developed. Ah Paw had preached over and over that foods needed to be balanced so that when ingested, their effect on the body would be balanced as well. The delicate relationship between ingredients had to be observed, as did the appearance of food, and its tastes. She had taught me to look and to feel as well as to taste. And I cooked what I had assimilated. I had no recipes, no cookbooks, nothing written down, only memories.

"Tau gung gam liu," she had said, waggling a finger at me, "You cannot take shortcuts." Always, she said, "Cook with patience, and with your heart." And, she would add, "Never substitute water for stock," a more figurative way of repeating that never should I seek shortcuts.

She had taught me that if I failed, I should try again. If what I set out to do was faulty, I should try a second time, and a third, if necessary. By the third time, she had said, it will turn out. Invariably it did. All of these sayings applied not only to cooking, but to life, Ah Paw said. *"Dai sik lam,"* or "Do not just sit and eat, and become lazy."

I believe all of this, and I try to live by it. When I cook, I adhere to the seasons. In winter, what I cook is intended to warm, to offset what is cold within us. In summer I cook foods that will cool. My Chinese foods are never eaten without thought. They have been shaped by more than 2,000 years of tradition, and I consider myself to be an inheritor, as well as a conduit, of this tradition. In my classes and in my writings I preach the purity of my cuisine. I guard it, and when I see it alloyed, it saddens me.

I have received a fair amount of recognition. My books have been praised and have won awards, and I have taught master classes, and have been the subject of articles on aspects of my cooking for major publications, national and international. I have been honored with lifetime achievement awards, and have conducted classes in my cooking all over the world, from Singapore to Helsinki. In addition to appearing on scores of television and radio programs, I have taught my cooking to many professional western chefs who desired knowledge of the Chinese kitchen.

None of this would have happened without the constant presence of Ah Paw, who is with me always. This may sound maudlin, or contrived, but I assure you, it is not. Her lessons, drummed into my head as a little girl, have never been forgotten. And, as I have grown older, I have come to realize how truly wise she was.

Over the years, I have come to think of her more frequently than I have the family into which I was born. When I learned of my mother's death in China, in 1975, my first thought was of Ah Paw, and how she would have wept over the death of her daughter. Perhaps it was because I learned of my mother's passing well after the fact,

MY FATHER (RIGHT) AND MY NUMBER-FOUR UNCLE, SHE SOOK, IN CANTON IN LATE 1984, SHORTLY BEFORE MY FATHER'S DEATH. THIS IS THE LAST PHOTOGRAPH TAKEN OF MY FATHER.

thirdhand, by telegram, sent by my father from Siu Lo Chun to his brother in Hong Kong, then on to me by sea mail. As I read my father's words, together with a request to send $300 to cover her funeral costs, I barely cried for this mother whom I had not seen for twenty-five years, but I did conjure up a sadness that I believe Ah Paw would have felt, had she been alive, over the death of her only daughter.

I did get to see my father in 1979 when, after China had opened its borders to Americans, my husband and I traveled to Guangzhou and by prearrangement met my father and a group of cousins in that city. I had not seen him for thirty years, since he left me in Hong Kong to return to Siu Lo Chun. He had been ill for some time, was enfeebled, and looked at my husband with some skepticism. But he warmed considerably when we showed him photographs of our three children. It was a short visit, without the permission of the Chinese government, and I left my father with photographs of his grandchildren, several boxes full of gifts, a radio and other things we thought he might wish for or need. I have a photograph of that meeting, which I keep. It turned out that that was the last time I would see him alive, for he died in 1985.

I learned of his death well after it occurred when, in December of that year during a visit to Hong Kong, a cousin informed me of it. He was the last of my family to pass away. My brother, mother, and father were dead, as was Ah Paw. There were no more ties, only memories, and the more distinct were, and are, of Ah Paw.

My thoughts of her are always pleasant. I picture her, afternoons, her hand on my supporting shoulder, as I help her walk to the small plaza of Sah Gau where she would sit and talk with other women of the town while I played. Often, I would merely pretend to play, for I would rather listen to her talk about her family members, including myself, and their health and wealth. She would talk about the next expected visit of her beloved nuns, and of the men in her family who had gone off to the United States to find money in its Golden Mountains and were sending support home.

The talk would be of harvests, hopefully good, of zodiac years. If the year was of the dragon, how many women in the various families were expecting, for the dragon was a marvelous birth omen. If a year of the snake, it was the duty of all of the women in the plaza to carry the message to the women of their families that it was not a year to become pregnant, nor to give birth, for the snake was the worst of birth omens.

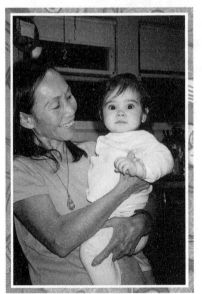

I remember her turning the pages of her astrological Tung Sing to determine which were the best days to travel, the best on which to plant, when to harvest, when to empty the ponds, when to take fish to market. The Tung Sing determined engagement and wedding dates, when the wedding cake was to be made and delivered to the groom's family. When the dowry was to be delivered, in particular the dried mushrooms and abalone, the dried sharkfins and birds' nests were to be delivered, for these were gifts of great honor.

Ah Fei, she would say, "Learn, learn, always learn. Never stop."

I never have, and I am teaching my granddaughter to do the same. The first soup she ever ate was made from Tianjin bok choy and chicken, an Ah Paw soup. Her first congee came directly, via me, from her great-grandmother's kitchen. Her first meat came from a chicken poached with Chinese herbs, later slices of roasted pork. Her vegetables were steamed in the Chinese way. Her first fruits were apples and pears, steamed, and pureed with their steaming juices.

My granddaughter is eating well. She will continue to do so, and she will learn. From her Ah Paw.

TEN

FOODS OF MY CHINESE KITCHEN:

INGREDIENT NOTES

FROM A TO Z

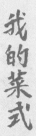

AS BEFITS A CUISINE WITH THE longest of histories, the basic foods of
China have changed little over the years, even over the centuries. So it is with the ingredients that I first cooked with in my grandmother's kitchen in Sah Gau, and which
I use today. Certainly, methods of cooking are altered by advances in equipment, but
the basic foods remain intact. What I cooked with then, I cook with now.

This is of course an advantage when one wishes, as I do, to be part of an historical context. The main difference, and a happy circumstance it is, is that these
traditional foods have become not only more widely available, but familiar. Huge supermarkets carrying Chinese and other Asian foodstuffs are commonplace these
days. Even familiar supermarkets, because of growing demand, stock shelves with
Chinese and Asian ingredients. Once rarities and difficult to find, these oils, spices,

condiments, prepared and preserved foods from China, Hong Kong, Taiwan, Singapore and countries elsewhere in Asia are no longer exotic.

A great many of these dried, preserved, pickled and otherwise prepared products are also available by mail order and through the Internet. Brands have also proliferated. Thus, securing the foods necessary to cook as I did in my grandmother's kitchen, and as I do now, is not difficult. What follows is an alphabetical list of those foods to be found in the recipes in this book. I describe them generically, mentioning brand names only when I believe that the one named is far superior to any other.

It should be noted that along with the growing number of brands and choices to be found, there have arisen many examples of fanciful, often misleading, labeling. A food can be described in many ways, so I urge caution when shopping. Alongside each ingredient is its name in Chinese characters. When shopping for specific foods, I suggest that you make a photocopy of the names of those items you wish, show this to the shopkeeper, and you will receive exactly what you wish.

Here, then, are the foods of my kitchen, the foods of my grandmother's kitchen, their descriptions, their properties, their care and storage. Cook with history.

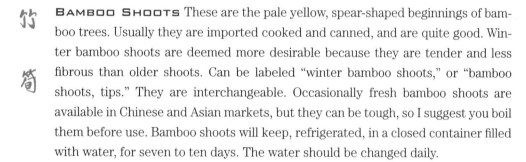

BAMBOO SHOOTS These are the pale yellow, spear-shaped beginnings of bamboo trees. Usually they are imported cooked and canned, and are quite good. Winter bamboo shoots are deemed more desirable because they are tender and less fibrous than older shoots. Can be labeled "winter bamboo shoots," or "bamboo shoots, tips." They are interchangeable. Occasionally fresh bamboo shoots are available in Chinese and Asian markets, but they can be tough, so I suggest you boil them before use. Bamboo shoots will keep, refrigerated, in a closed container filled with water, for seven to ten days. The water should be changed daily.

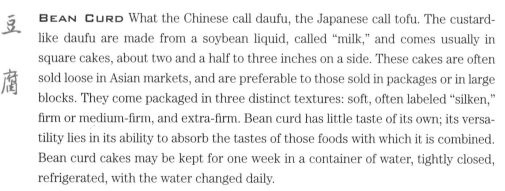

BEAN CURD What the Chinese call daufu, the Japanese call tofu. The custard-like daufu are made from a soybean liquid, called "milk," and comes usually in square cakes, about two and a half to three inches on a side. These cakes are often sold loose in Asian markets, and are preferable to those sold in packages or in large blocks. They come packaged in three distinct textures: soft, often labeled "silken," firm or medium-firm, and extra-firm. Bean curd has little taste of its own; its versatility lies in its ability to absorb the tastes of those foods with which it is combined. Bean curd cakes may be kept for one week in a container of water, tightly closed, refrigerated, with the water changed daily.

BEAN CURD, RED WET PRESERVED These are cubes of bean curd, red in color, which have been allowed to ferment usually in a mix of salt, sugar, rice wine and the liquid from red rice, which gives the cubes their color. The cubes come in crocks and jars labeled variously "wet bean curd," "red wet bean curd" or "fermented bean curd." This bean curd is not spicy, but adds flavor and the distinctive red color to the barbeques and braised dishes in which it is used. Available in Asian markets, ask for it phonetically as *Lam Yue*.

BEAN SAUCE This is a thick puree made from the soybeans that remain after soy sauce has been manufactured and poured off, and thus is fermented. They are mixed with wheat flour, salt and sugar, resulting in a coarse brown sauce that contains pieces of soybeans. There is also a mix labeled "ground bean sauce," which means simply that they have been ground into a mash. You may also see jars labeled "yellow bean sauce," or "brown bean sauce," but they are the same. After opening, the jar should be kept refrigerated. The bean sauce will keep four to six months.

BEAN SAUCE, HOT This is made from pureed soybeans, blended with salt, sugar, sesame oil and hot peppers into a reddish-brown mixture. It is quite good, quite spicy. After opening, the jar should be kept refrigerated. The bean sauce will keep four to six months.

BEAN SPROUTS There are two varieties of these sprouts. Mung bean sprouts are grown from mung beans. They are white and plump, with crunch, and are sold by weight in Asian markets. Stored, refrigerated, in plastic bags in which holes have been punched, they will keep for no more than two days. Soybean sprouts, also white, but longer than mung bean sprouts, have soybeans growing on their tips. Not as widely available as mung bean sprouts, they can be stored the same way.

BEAN THREADS These are often called "bean thread noodles" or "vermicelli bean threads," or "cellophane noodles." They are made when mung beans are moistened, mashed, strained, and formed into very thin white noodles. They come dried, in ½-pound packages, divided into four two-ounce bundles. Stored tightly wrapped and in a cool place, they will keep indefinitely.

豆

豉

BLACK BEANS, FERMENTED Fragrant black beans, preserved in salt, come either in plastic-wrapped packs or cardboard cartons. They are flavored lightly with ginger and orange peel. Before using, the salt must be rinsed off. They will keep for as long as a year, without refrigeration, if they are in a tightly sealed container.

白

菜

BOK CHOY Probably China's most recognizable vegetable. Its name translates as "white vegetable" because of it white bulbous stalk, which contrasts with its deep green leaves. Native to China, variations of it exist in different parts of China and in other parts of Asia. In Chinatown markets, smaller "baby bok choy" are usually available; in Western markets, the larger version is usually sold. Bok choy is most versatile because of its crispness and inherent sweetness. Though often referred to, in error, as "Chinese cabbage," it bears no relation to cabbage. Bok choy will keep no more than four days in the vegetable drawer of a refrigerator, but it tends to lose its sweetness quickly, and its leaves begin to yellow.

杞

子

BOXTHORN SEEDS These are not seeds, but the tiny, red, raisinlike fruit of the boxthorn shrub. They have a faint, mildly sweet taste that can enhance the flavor of soups. They are considered restoratives, and helpful to eye health. Once available only in herbal shops, they are now available, packaged, in Chinese groceries and online. Often labeled "wolfberries," more familiarly, "boxthorn." The young leaves of its shrub are often stir-fried, as are the seeds, and are added to soups. Even the boxthorn twig is used to make soups, or infusions, prized by the elderly as bone strengtheners. These seeds, kept in a tightly closed container, in a cool place, will keep four to six months.

辣

椒

CHILES The best, in my view, are Thai chiles, colored deep red or deep green, about 1½ inches long. They are quite hot and impart a heat to the mouth that lingers, yet they are pleasant. I also find them dependable in terms of numbers used to achieve degrees of hotness. They will keep, refrigerated, for ten days to two weeks in an open container, lightly covered with plastic wrap. Do not seal the container, for the chiles will deteriorate. They maybe dried as well, but their heat is less intense.

CHINESE CHIVES Also known as "garlic chives," these are more pungent than the customary western chives. They are wider and flatter, though of the same green color. Yellow chives are the same vegetable, but as they grow they are deprived of sunlight and thus become lighter. Their taste is milder than that of green chives. If unavailable, use scallions in their place, but the taste will differ. These should be used fresh. They will keep no longer than one or two days.

CHINESE EGGPLANT This bright lavender to purple eggplant, often white-tinged, is narrower than its western counterpart and usually no more than 2 inches in diameter at its thickest. Its taste is similar to the more familiar eggplant, but its skin is quite thin and tender, and need not be removed before cooking. This eggplant should be refrigerated and eaten fresh. After two or three days their skins begin to show brown spots, and they tend to lose their sweetness.

CHINESE TURNIPS These large white vegetables range from fourteen to sixteen inches in length, often longer, and are two to three inches in diameter at their thickest point. They have crispness and can be as hot as radishes. They will keep for one week in a refrigerator vegetable drawer, but are best used promptly.

CHOI SUM A leafy vegetable with thin, tender stalks. It is totally green, from its large outside leaves, to the smaller inside leaves, to the light green stalks, which are crisp and sweet. Choi sum, like other leafy vegetables, tends to lose its sweetness, so it should be eaten as soon after purchase as possible. They will keep, refrigerated no more than two to three days, after which their leaves turn brown and they lose their taste.

CORIANDER This aromatic leaf, or *yuen sai*, is also called "fresh coriander" to distinguish it from the spice seeds, as well as "Chinese parsley" and "cilantro." It is similar only in appearance to parsley. It has an intense smell and a distinctive taste, used either as an ingredient or a garnish. Suggestions that Italian parsley be used as a substitute are without merit. Their aromas and tastes are markedly different. There is no substitute for coriander, which should be used fresh, so that its bouquet will be appreciated. It may be refrigerated for a week at most.

EGGS, PRESERVED The eggs most often preserved in China are duck eggs, the most common of which are called "thousand-year-old eggs." They are considerably younger than their name says. Raw duck eggs are wrapped usually with a pasty mix of salt, tea leaves, rice husks and a preservative, sodium bicarbonate, and allowed to cure for fifty days. The shell becomes mottled gray, the inside of the egg like aspic, the yolk a deep, dull green, the white a deep brown. These eggs used to be shipped in earthenware crocks. Now they are packed, six to a package, labeled "preserved duck eggs." They are often eaten as they are, sliced and accompanied by pickled ginger, and in congees and soups. A cautionary note: As these eggs age their insides tend to shrink and dry. They should be kept refrigerated, for about 2 weeks.

EIGHT-STAR ANISE These are the tiny eight-pointed hard star fruit of the Chinese anise tree. Also called "star anise," their flavor is more pronounced than that of anise seed. They should be kept in a tightly sealed jar in a cool, dry place, and will keep six months, though their intensity and flavor will gradually ebb.

FIVE-SPICE SEASONING The five spices in this mix can be any combination of eight-star anise, fennel seeds, cinnamon, cloves, ginger, licorice, nutmeg and Sichuan peppercorns. Different manufacturers prefer different mixtures, though the anise and cinnamon tend to be dominant. You may devise your personal five-spice mixture by having it mixed at a herbalist shop. Often the spices are ground into powder that is quite pungent, and should be used sparingly. The mixture is used to flavor foods such as soybean cakes, barbecued pork, stews and long-cooked dishes. Care for this seasoning as you would eight-star anise.

FLOUR There are, to be sure, countless brands of flour in the markets, but I have determined, after many tests and trials, that one commercial flour is best to use in making breads and dim sum doughs: Gold Medal All-Purpose Flour, Enriched, Bleached. There are, in the Chinese kitchen, other flours, starches and powders that are essentially milled flours. These are listed separately.

GINGER This is also referred to as "gingerroot." It flavors foods quite well. When selecting gingerroots, look for thick roots with smooth outer skins, because ginger tends to wrinkle and roughen with age. In addition to providing flavor, it serves to diffuse strong fish and shellfish odors. It should be used sparingly and should be sliced, often peeled, before use. Its strength is often dictated by its preparation. I use ginger sliced, peeled and unpeeled, lightly smashed, julienned, minced and shredded. When placed in a heavy brown paper bag and stored on a shelf in a refrigerator, it will keep two weeks. There is also so-called young ginger, which is very smooth, slightly pink in color, without the tough skin of older ginger, and quite crisp. It is often called "spring ginger," as well, but this is a misnomer, for it is available year-round. I use this young ginger to make my ginger pickle. In recent years a "yellow ginger" from China has come on the market. These roots are yellower in color, their flavor more pungent.

GINGER JUICE Although this is available in small bottles, a better-quality ginger juice can be made at home. It is simple and quick to make. Grate peeled ginger into a bowl, then press it through a garlic press. Make as needed. Its shelf life, refrigerated, is two days.

GINGKO NUTS These hard-shelled nuts are the seeds of the gingko tree, a common shade tree in China. They are shaped like tiny footballs, pale yellow when raw, they become translucent when cooked. They must be cooked before being eaten, and are available fresh or canned. When fresh, with shells on, they require cooking. Those in cans, shelled, are already cooked. Raw nuts in shells will keep, refrigerated, in a plastic bag for four weeks. Cooked ginkgo will keep for only four to five days. Canned nuts, when opened, should be used within a week. Both canned and raw gingkos should be refrigerated.

GLUTINOUS RICE This short-grained rice is often called "sweet rice" and "sticky rice." When cooked, its gluten makes its kernels stick together in a mass instead of separating the way extra-long-grain rice does. It is often labeled "sweet rice." One of its best uses is in making congee, where it is mixed with another short-grained rice with less gluten. There are also black glutinous and long-grained glutinous rices. The black rice is often used to make sweets, particularly in Southeast Asia.

GLUTINOUS RICE POWDER This finely ground dried glutinous rice is used in making steamed rice cakes and as a base for dumplings. It is also known as "glutinous rice flour."

HOISIN SAUCE A thick deep-brown, sweetened sauce made from pureed soybeans, garlic, sugar and chiles. Some brands add a bit of vinegar as well, others thicken the mixture with flour. Often it is referred to, erroneously, as "plum sauce," which it most certainly is not. Hoisin sauce comes in jars. Once opened, the jar should be refrigerated. It will keep two to three months.

JICAMA Known in Chinese as *sah gut*, this bulbous root is sweet and crisp, with a sand-colored exterior and a white interior. It may be eaten raw or cooked. In Mexico and the Southwest its name reflects its origins, but it has become widely cultivated in China and elsewhere in Asia. It is a fine substitute for fresh water chestnuts. Stored in a brown paper bag, refrigerated, it will stay crisp for three to four days.

KETCHUP Ketchup from China comes in bottles. It is made from tomatoes, vinegar and varied spices. The difference between ketchup from China and that in the West is that Chinese use it more as a coloring agent than for its flavor. Chinese ketchup can be found in Chinatown markets, but if unavailable use the Western kind. It is believed by some that ketchup originated in China. In southern China, on the island of Amoy, there is a mixture of fish essence and soy sauce called *keh chap*, that is believed to have been a precursor.

LOTUS LEAVES These large leaves of the lotus plant, sold dried, are used as food wrappings. The leaves impart a distinctive, and pleasant aroma to the foods they are wrapped around, after being moistened. In China, we always had access to fresh lotus leaves, but these are rare in the United States, where usually only dried lotus leaves are available. Once only sold commercially to restaurants, lotus leaves are now packaged in smaller amounts and can be found in Chinese and Asian markets. These dried leaves will keep indefinitely, and even as they become more brittle with age, they are resuscitated after being soaked in water, but as they age they lose some of their inherent aroma.

LOTUS ROOT This gourd-shaped root of the lotus often grows four or five together, connected like a string of sausages, each four to five inches long and three inches in diameter. When the root is cut across, there is a pattern of holes not unlike that of Swiss cheese. Their texture is crisp and dry, and they should be kept refrigerated in a brown bag and used quickly, since they tend to turn brown and lose their crispness and flavor quickly.

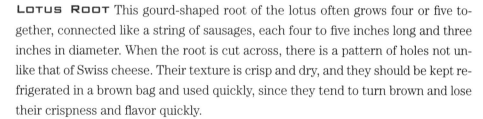

LOTUS SEED PASTE This deep red-brown paste is made from the olive-shaped seeds of the lotus plant pod cooked with sugar. The cooked paste is used mainly as filling for pastries and for special sweets such as moon cakes. The many brands of paste comes in cans, generally all of equal quality. Once removed from the can, the paste will keep, refrigerated, in a closed container, for two months.

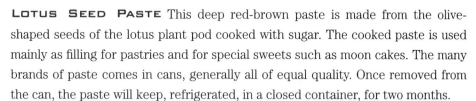

MUSHROOMS, CHINESE BLACK These dried mushrooms come in boxes, cellophane packages, or loose. They are black, dark gray, or speckled black and gray and their caps range in size from about that of a nickel to three inches in diameter. Those in boxes are the choicest, both in size and color, and are priced accordingly. They are referred to in China as "flower mushrooms," thick and meaty. Chinese black mushrooms must always be soaked in hot water for at least twenty minutes before use, their stems discarded, and the undersides of their caps should be thoroughly rinsed and squeezed dry. Dried, they will keep indefinitely, at room temperature in a tightly closed container. If you live in a damp or humid climate they should be kept frozen. These are the same mushrooms known outside of China as "shiitakes." I prefer them dried rather than fresh, for the intensity of their flavor. If you cannot get dried black mushrooms, use fresh ones.

 NOODLES There are many variations on the noodle in China, all known collectively as *mein*. There are wheat flour noodles, fresh, fried and dried, of various widths, made from flour either just mixed with water or with eggs added. There are rice noodles, also fresh and dried, of various widths. Very fine rice noodles are often labeled "rice sticks." There are even so-called mung bean noodles, which are simply another name for bean threads. For most Chinese noodle dishes, most varieties of Western noodles will be quite suitable. For example, vermicelli, capellini and angel hair pastas will do nicely as substitutes for very fine wheat noodles. There are no substitutes for rice noodles. As with all noodles, those fresh and soft should be used as soon as possible; those dried will keep indefinitely.

 OILS Peanut oil is the preferred oil of the Chinese kitchen, and surely of mine, not only for its inherently healthy properties, but for the nuttiness it imparts to dishes. Peanut oils from China and Hong Kong emit a more intense aroma and flavor than do domestic peanut oils. For all of the recipes in this book, you may use canola, corn or soybean oil as well as other vegetable oils, but the flavors they will impart will be quite different. If I had to choose one alternative, it would be canola. Never use olive oil as a substitute, for the high heat necessary to cook most Chinese dishes will cause the olive oil to smoke and burn too quickly.

 OYSTER SAUCE This sauce is based upon oysters that have been boiled and dried, cooked into thickness, then ground. It is a highly prized versatile seasoning, not only for its distinctive taste, but for the richness of its deep brown color. There are many brands, but I prefer the Hop Sing Lung oyster sauce from Hong Kong. Once open, a bottle should be refrigerated and will keep four months. Unrefrigerated, it will also keep for a good period of time if used often and quickly. I prefer to refrigerate it.

  PRESERVED MUSTARD These are preserved mustard plants that have been cooked, preserved in salt and sugar, then dried. It is called *mui choi* in China. Brown in color, and put into plastic bags, it is soft and pliable, and is used in steaming, stir-frying, braising, and in soups. This is often labeled "salted mustard." It is often sold loose as well. Often tiny salt crystals can be seen on the preserved mustard, but it does not affect its taste. It should be stored in a sealed jar, at room temperature, and will keep six months. The longer it is kept, the darker it becomes. Before use the leaves must be opened and the salt and grit thoroughly removed by washing.

RED BEANS These small, deep-red beans are generally used in sweets, or sweet soups, although occasionally they are combined with other foods in casseroles. They are sold in plastic sacks, by weight and will keep for six months in a closed container. The most frequently used form of red beans is in a paste. The beans are soaked and boiled, then mashed and cooked with sugar, and finally mashed with either lard or peanut oil into a paste. The paste, which comes in cans, is used as fillings for pastries, buns and dumplings. Once opened, the paste should be kept refrigerated, in a closed compartment. It will keep four to six weeks.

RED DATES These dried fruits come in plastic-wrapped packages labeled either "red dates" or "dried dates." Do not buy pitted, for they lose taste after being pitted. Once opened and removed from the package they should be placed in a glass jar, covered and stored in a cool place. They will keep six months.

RICE Rice is the Chinese universal, particularly in the south, where it is the core of every meal. Its varieties are many. Rice in China is short-, medium- and long-grain, with extra-long-grain rice considered the finest. The kernels of short-grain rices, of which glutinous rice is one, tend to be stubby and contain much starch. Medium-grain rices are slightly longer, with a bit less starch. Extra-long-grain rice kernels are just that: long, with little residual starch. Cooked, the kernels separate and the rice becomes fluffy. Short-grain rices tend to clump together when cooked, as do most medium-grain rices. The best of the extra-long-grains are grown domestically in the south, particularly in Texas, and there are jasmine-scented extra-long-grains from Thailand that are excellent. Rice, as a crop, is *mai*; cooked as a food, it is *fan*.

Other varieties include brown rice, which is partially milled rice in which the brown husk is left on the kernel; red rice, grown near the Chinese-Thai border, a rice used chiefly as a colorant; and black rices, particularly a glutinous variety used to make sweets in Southeast Asia. Rices may be stored indefinitely, in covered containers, in cool, dry places.

RICE POWDER This finely ground powder of short-grain rice, is called "white rice powder," flour or starch. It is used, often in combination with glutinous rice powder, to make savory and sweet cakes. This powder, when mixed with milk, is used often as a substitute for mother's milk. Store as you would any flour.

ROCK SUGAR This is a compound of white sugar, raw brown sugar and honey. Also at times labeled "rock candy," it is used in sweet soups and in teas. It comes in one-pound sacks and resembles a collection of small amber rocks. Stored in a tightly sealed jar it will keep indefinitely.

SAUSAGES, CHINESE The most popular Chinese sausages are traditionally made of diced pork and pork fat, and are called *lop cheung*. There is also a sausage of pork livers wrapped around pork fat called *yon cheung*, or liver sausage. These sausages are cured, but not cooked, and are generally sold loose, in links, by weight. But there are, as well, *lop cheung* of ground pork, sold in one-pound packages, which can be found in refrigerated market compartments. As noted, all of these sausages must be cooked before eating. They may be kept, refrigerated, for about a month, or frozen for three months.

SESAME OIL This most aromatic of oils is made from pressed, often toasted, sesame seeds. It has a defined nutlike aroma. I prefer to use it as an additive to sauces and marinades or as a dressing. I do not recommend cooking with it, for it tends to burn quickly. When this occurs there is no benefit to be had from its generally fine aroma and little of its taste. Adding a bit of sesame oil as a finish to an already prepared dish imparts fine flavor, to some soups and in particular to a steamed fish. In China and Japan, sesame oil is thick and brown; in the Middle East it is thinner and lighter. I recommend sesame oil from China. Stored in a tightly closed bottle at room temperature, it will keep about four months.

SESAME SEEDS, BLACK AND WHITE Black sesame seeds, either roasted or not, are used customarily as a pastry decoration, or as an ingredient in sweet pastry fillings. Roasted white sesame seeds are used generally in dumpling fillings, as garnishes, or occasionally as an ingredient in sweets.

Seeds are used mostly after being dry-roasted. *To dry-roast sesame seeds:* Heat wok over high heat, thirty seconds. Add seeds, stir, lower heat to medium, stir for 1 minute. Lower heat to low, cook for another minute, until seeds release their fragrance. Turn off heat. Seeds are ready for use.

I prefer keeping sesame seeds, both raw and roasted, in the freezer, since they have a tendency to become rancid. Frozen, they will keep at least 1 year.

SESAME SEED PASTE This paste is made by mixing ground white sesame seeds with soybean oil. It comes in jars and is smooth, with the consistency of peanut butter. Its sesame taste is quite pronounced. After opening, the jar should be refrigerated. It will keep six months. There is also a sesame seed paste from the Middle East known as tahini. I find it milder and less intense, than that from China.

 SHAO-HSING WINE This rice-based wine is made in China and Taiwan, and comes in differing degrees of alcohol. From China, I use not only the basic Shao-Hsing with which to cook, but also its best refined grade, labeled "Hua Tiao Chiew." From Taiwan, I cook with a brand called "Shao-Hsing V.O." Both have distinctive sherrylike flavors, with that of the Taiwan Shao-Hsing slightly more intense. When shopping for Shao-Hsing you may simply ask for *far jiu*, a generic term, like asking for "burgundy." But take care not to buy any bottle that indicates that it is a "cooking wine," for the wine will have an inferior taste.

As you've seen in this book I use Shao-Hsing widely, in marinades, sauces or on its own, for it adds greatly, in whatever use. A medium-dry sherry, such as an Amontillado, will substitute nicely.

 SHRIMP, DRIED These are cooked and shelled shrimp of various sizes, dried and salted for preservation. They come loose, sold by weight, or packaged. Before use, they should be soaked in warm water for at least twenty minutes. They will keep two to three months, refrigerated, in a tightly closed container. They can also be frozen for storage. They should be orange-pink in color, and a sure sign that they are aging and losing their strength and taste is a change to a grayish color.

 SICHUAN PEPPERCORNS These are quite different from the peppercorns with which most people are familiar. They are reddish, not solid, opened like tiny buds. Often called "flower peppercorns" because of their appearance, they are neither hot, nor peppery. Instead, they're rather mild. Store them in a tightly closed jar as you would ordinary peppercorns. Several recipes call for ground peppercorns. You must pulverize them yourself. Store ground peppercorns in a closed jar as well. They will keep for about six months.

 SILK SQUASH A thin, cucumber-shaped gourd, with pronounced ridges running along its length. It is deep green, but its flesh is white, with a faint sweetness, and a soft texture. It is excellent in soups. Use it quickly, at its freshest, within two days.

Snow Peas These are the tender, and distinctively sweet, pods of the snow pea vine. They are used in stir-fries and soups, but both ends must be snapped off, their strings removed, before cooking. Their vine leaves, or shoots, called *dau miu*, are quite sweet on their own, when sauteed. The snow peas will keep no more than three to four days, and should be eaten quickly to enjoy their taste.

Sour Mustard Pickle This leafy cabbagelike vegetable, with large, round, green-tinged, bulbous stalks, is also known as "mustard greens," and by the Chinese as *kai choi*, or "leaf-mustard cabbage." Its taste is strong, and it is used fresh in soups or stir-fried with meats, but is more commonly used in its preserved form. Water-blanched, and cured with salt, sugar and vinegar, it is used as well in stir-fries and soups. Its heart is often a garnish. It can be bought, already cured, in large crocks, loose, by weight, or in cans labeled "sour mustard pickle," or "sour mustard greens," or "mustard greens." If you buy the greens loose, place them in a tightly closed plastic container, refrigerated. They will keep three months. Once cans are opened, greens should be stored in the same manner, and will have the same storage life.

Soy Sauce This sauce, a tradition of Chinese cooking for 3,000 years, is the product of the fermentation of soybeans, mixed with wheat flour, water and salt. It comes in light and dark varieties. The light soys are taken from the tops of batches being prepared, usually in earthenware crocks, the dark soys from the bottoms. The best soy sauces are fermented naturally in the sun, not indoors in factories. I prefer the soy sauces from Hong Kong and China to all others, including those produced in the United States and Japan, which I find a bit thin and too salty.

Dark Soys, which include such label distinctions as "dark" "double dark," and a quite thick and dark "pearl" sauce, are best for imparting a rich color to a prepared dish. Some dark soys even have molasses added. I prefer dark soys with meats. The sauces I regard as superior are made in Hong Kong's Koon Chun Sauce Factory. Its double-dark soy is labeled "Koon Chun Double Black Soy Sauce."

There is another dark soy I prefer, one to which mushrooms have been added, for additional sweetness. It comes from China and is labeled "Pearl River Bridge Mushroom Soy."

生
柚
酒
類

Light Soys are noted for their somewhat sweeter taste and marry well with chicken, fish and other seafood. The Koon Chun Sauce Factory's light soy, also superior, and my most recommended light soy sauce, is labeled "Koon Chun Thin Soy Sauce."

Most soys come in bottles and, tightly capped, will keep for six months at room temperature. Not only is soy sauce an additive, it is often used as a dip. In general the Chinese use soy sauce more sparingly than do Westerners.

SPIRITS In China both spirits and traditional wines share the generic name *chiew*, so long as the product contains alcohol. Thus wines, fermented spirits, even beers, are *chiew*. Even the Shao-Hsing wine discussed earlier is a *chiew*. I have given Shao-Hsing its own place in this ingredients list because of its prominence and the considerable use I make of it.

I also use "Chinese white rice wine" variously. There are four grades of this crystal-clear very white wine. The first is *soi chiew*, a somewhat humorous name that translates as "water wine." It is weak and its main use is as a disposable temple offering. Second is *mai chiew*, or simply "rice wine," a bit stronger, but without character. The third, which I recommend for the recipes in this book, is labeled "Pearl River Bridge, Kiu Kuang Shuang Jin Chiew," in which the words *shuang jin* translate as "double-steamed," to indicate a superior grade. Fourth is *san cheng chiew*, or triple-steamed, and very strong, which I do not recommend for cooking.

The other spirit mentioned in this book is "Mei Kuei Lu Chiew," a very special liquor from Tianjin. Its name, translated as "rose dew chiew," is based upon sorghum, with the addition of a liquor made from soaked rose petals, soaked, the Chinese say, only in dew. It is quite like a smooth eau-de-vie.

As a substitute in recipes for both the rice wine and this rose petal *chiew*, I specify gin—one gin in particular. It is "No. 209," to denote the number of its registered San Francisco distillery, and made by the Napa Valley winemaker Leslie Rudd. It is a soft and elegant gin, fragrant with such botanicals as juniper berries from Tuscany, Chinese cassia bark, cardamom from Guatemala, bergamot orange from Calabria and coriander seeds from central Europe. This little United Nations of flavors produces a truly lovely gin with which to cook.

SPRING ROLL SKINS These thin, cooked skins are white in color and contain no eggs. Once square, now they are usually round, about six to seven inches in diameter, depending upon the brand. They are found in refrigerated compartments of markets. Usually freshly made, they will keep no more than two to three days, refrigerated. They may be frozen, wrapped first in plastic, then foil and finally in a plastic sack. They will keep frozen two to three months.

春
卷
皮

SUGARCANE SUGAR These are firm, layered, caramel-colored blocks made from sugarcane. They come usually wrapped in plastic packages and occasionally loose, in crocks. They are sold by weight. Stored in a tightly closed jar, at room temperature, these blocks will keep six months. The blocks will darken as they age.

TANGERINE PEEL, DRIED This dried, wrinkled, hard brown skin of the tangerine is used to flavor. The darker the peel, the older and the older the better. The oldest dried tangerine peels are also the most expensive. They are sold in packages and wrapped. Stored in a cool place, they will keep indefinitely. You can also dry your own. Place peel on a cookie sheet and allow to sit under the sun until hard and dry, two to three days.

TAPIOCA STARCH Also called "tapioca flour," or "tapioca powder," this is made from the starch of the cassava root. Much of it comes packaged from Thailand, and is used as a basic ingredient in dumpling doughs. It is used for dusting or coating foods and occasionally as a sauce thickener in place of cornstarch. Once opened, the starch should be kept in a closed container at room temperature. It will keep six to nine months.

TARO ROOT The starchy root of the taro plant. Taro is somewhat like a potato but is more fibrous and is tinged throughout by tiny purple threads. It must be eaten cooked and is usually steamed or boiled. As it steams it emits a chestnutlike aroma. After cooking it can be mashed. It can be stir-fried in its raw state. Refrigerated, it will keep no more than two to three days.

TIANJIN BOK CHOY This is often called "Tianjin cabbage," or "Tientsin bok choy," for the present and past spellings of its native city, or "celery cabbage," or "Napa cabbage." There are two varieties, one with a long stalk, another round and leafy. The latter is the sweeter of the two and my preference. It may be kept refrigerated in a plastic bag for about four days. After that it loses its sweetness, so it should be eaten early.

TIGER LILY BUDS These are elongated, reddish brown lily buds that have been dried. They are also known to the Chinese as "golden needles." The best are pliable. When dry and brittle, they are too old. Sold in packages, they will keep at least three months in a tightly covered jar in a cool place.

VINEGARS Several Chinese vinegars are used in this book, the most distinctive of which is *Chinkiang vinegar*. It is reddish-black, very strong, made from glutinous rice. It has a distinct, direct taste and an aroma faintly reminiscent of a commercial balsamic. There are many brands, generally equal in quality.

 There is also a distinctive black, sweet rice vinegar with sugar, ginger and cloves added. It's a special vinegar used for the pigs' feet and boiled egg dish traditionally eaten by Chinese women after giving birth. I prefer the Koon Chun Sauce Company's variety from Hong Kong. This vinegar can also be combined with Chinkiang to create a more potent vinegar.

Red vinegar is made from distilled vinegar, diluted with water and with red coloring added. My preference for that is also from Koon Chun in Hong Kong, very much like a red wine vinegar, which may be used in its place.

White vinegar is distilled from a mixture of rice, sorghum and corn. I prefer two brands, "Dragon Fountain Grain Vinegar" and "Swatow Rice Vinegar," both imported from China. If unavailable, use distilled white vinegar as a substitute.

 WATER CHESTNUTS These are not nuts, despite their name. They are bulbs, purplish-brown, that grow in muddy water. The meat of the water chestnut is white, crisp and juicy, delicious even when raw. To peel fresh water chestnuts is time-consuming, but the results are its reward. I prefer that canned water chestnuts not be used, except in water chestnut cake. The best substitute is jicama, for its crispness. Water chestnuts should be eaten as quickly as possible, for they lose their firmness with age, and begin to deteriorate. They may be kept, with their skins and dirt remnants intact, in a brown paper bag, on a refrigerated shelf, for one week to ten days. If they have been washed, keep them similarly and for the same amount of time. If you have peeled them, wash and dry them, place in a bowl, cover with plastic wrap, and refrigerate. These will keep two to three days.

 WATER CHESTNUT POWDER Like other ground and milled products, this powder is basically a flour. It is used to make cakes, or to thicken sauces. Store as you would any flour. It will keep up to one year.

 WHEAT STARCH This finely ground substance is what remains of wheat flour when the wheat's protein has been removed to make gluten. In this book it is used as an ingredient for vegetarian eggs, but it is also used in making dim sum skins and fillings. Kept in a closed container, in a cool place, this will keep three to six months.

WINTERMELON A large melon that looks quite like a watermelon from the out-side. Its rind is dark green, occasionally mottled, while its interior is white with a pale green tinge and contains white seeds. The melon has no taste of its own, but absorbs the tastes of whatever it is cooked with. When it is cooked, usually in soup, or steamed, the melon flesh becomes translucent. Often, as is done in this book, the whole melon serves as a tureen, with stock, flavorings and other ingredients added after the melon has been hollowed out. Wintermelon should be used imme-diately, for it tends to dry out quickly, particularly when pieces are cut from it. It is sold variously as a whole melon, or in pieces, by weight.

 WON TON SKINS Also labeled occasionally as "won ton wrappers," often spelled "won tun," these thin skins are made from wheat flour, eggs, water and bak-ing soda. They also come without eggs. Packaged in one-pound stacks, they are square, either 3½ inches, or 3¼ inches on a side. Depending upon their thickness and size there will be sixty to eighty skins per package. They will keep refrigerated two to three days, and may be frozen for two to three months. To freeze, double-wrap them first in plastic, then with foil, then finally in a plastic bag, for better preservation.

EAT DRINK MAN WOMAN
by Fred Ferretti

WHAT ENSURED—I MIGHT SAY SANCTIONED—my engagement to my future wife was my willingness to eat the bulbous eye of a fat fish, a garoupa, that had been steamed in my honor by her number-six aunt. When I first met the woman I first knew as Yin-Fei Lo in 1958 in the fabric shop she managed, she gave me a glass of iced sour-lemon squash to counter the humid blasts of the Hong Kong summer. Our first formal date was a chaperoned restaurant lunch, during which a family friend glared at me as we ate our fried pork chops and Hong Kong's spongy version of strawberry shortcake. Within ten days I was telling her, over cups of tepid, sweetened coffee in a teahouse, that I would soon return to marry her—a pronouncement that elicited some skepticism on her part.

In 1959, after I had been discharged from the Army, I returned to Hong Kong to

EILEEN AND FRED, ON A TRIP TO BALI.

do just that. The significance of our wedding reception in a waterfront hotel rested in the occasion it celebrated, but just as surely in the foods set out for our guests: crisp chicken, symbolizing the phoenix and rebirth; suckling pig, a wedding constant, for among the Chinese it signifies innocence and purity; a steamed fish, indicating that life will proceed smoothly, forever; oysters, for good fortune; shrimp, because the word for it, *har*, sounds like joyous laughter; and finally, tangerines and oranges, the seeds of which were assurances that children would proceed from our marriage. Everything of personal import between my wife and me, everything—from our first meeting to our current careers—has food at its core, a circumstance not only of continuing pleasure, but of constant bond.

Yin-Fei grew up in Sun Tak, a Cantonese agricultural area that was, and is, a shrine to cookery. The Chinese say that "if you are born in Sun Tak, you are born to cook." And so she was. Because her family wished it so—"My mother said it would be easier to please a husband if I could cook"—she began cooking at the age of five, most often in the kitchen of her maternal grandmother, her "Ah Paw." Ah Paw's wealth and bound feet meant that she never went to market, or even ventured into a kitchen. However, her knowledge of food—its preparation and its place in the family and social structure—was enormous and compelling.

The belief in food as more than mere nourishment was reinforced by her number-six aunt, with whom Yin-Fei eventually went to live in Hong Kong after she fled China's revolution as a twelve-year-old. It was in Hong Kong that Yin-Fei later added Eileen to her Chinese name, which translates as "Flying Swallow."

Each of my wife's ten cookbooks has centered upon a different aspect of Chinese cookery, always in a cultural context. Writers and critics have given Eileen such labels as "the Cantonese Julia Child," "the Chinese Alice Waters," "the Chinese Marcella Hazan" and "the Diva of Dim Sum." I prefer that she be recognized for the unique person she is, a woman of great talent who has devoted her professional life to teaching, preaching and practicing what is proper, pure and traditional in the cuisine of her native land.

In her writing, teaching and television, radio and public appearances, reverence for things that grow is another recurring theme, as is the need to respect the essential nature of ingredients when cooking them.

Eileen has an inner strength that belies her diminutive size. Four-foot-nine-and-one-half inches in height ("Don't forget the half inch," she has warned me), she weighs in at less than one hundred pounds. I recall our daughter, Elena, once exhorting an unhappy college roommate to think more positively, saying, "Look at my mother. She doesn't know she's four-foot-nine." And a half.

I discovered early in our relationship that Eileen cares deeply about the foods she cooks and serves. As she does so, she gives wholly of herself—she loves. Nor should this be construed as simple metaphor. To my wife, food is love, tangibly. For example, Elena, a television producer, might mention in a phone call that she is tired or fighting a cold. This information will occasion a day's work in the kitchen for Eileen and a delivery to Elena's apartment of soups, stews, bowls of noodles, slabs of turnip cake, the breaded cauliflower she likes. Why? "It will make her better."

Our younger son, Stephen, a sports coach and executive, will visit our home after a practice to find a buffet of his favorites: spicy shredded beef with vegetables; roast Peking Duck with pancakes and *muy choi deuk jee yuk*, a chopped pork and preserved vegetable dish that he has enjoyed since before he could talk.

Our older son, Christopher, a teaching chef at the French Culinary Institute, brings over his creations from cooking school: pureed lentil soup, apple tart, a black currant sorbet in a port wine reduction. He smiles with pleasure, and relief, when Eileen pronounces his efforts edible.

After Eileen and I came to the United States and settled into our New York City apartment, my mother and father—in an effort to put their new daughter-in-law at ease—took us to their neighborhood Chinese restaurant. Despite food that, to be charitable, was neither Chinese nor good, it was a momentous night; my father mastered the skill of eating with chopsticks, even managing ice cream and fortune cookies with them. And only once after that did he ever forget himself and ask for bread and butter at a Chinese meal.

Eileen honored her new parents-in-law by asking my mother how to cook Italian dishes. In fact, my wife's adaptation of my mother's pasta, sausages and meatballs recipes was infinitely richer than the original—an observation I never made in my mother's presence.

There is one particular dish that Eileen cooks often—actually, the first Chinese food she ever prepared for us in our new home—that I have come to regard as a continuing gift, an affirmation of us together. Here is her recipe.

Beef with Peppers and Black Beans

(See Jiu Chau Ngau)

豉
椒
炒
牛

MARINADE

1½ tablespoons oyster sauce

1½ teaspoons sesame oil

1 teaspoon ginger juice mixed with 2 teaspoons Shao-Hsing wine, or sherry

1 teaspoon dark soy sauce

1½ teaspoons sugar

½ teaspoon salt

⅛ teaspoon white pepper

2 teaspoons cornstarch

1¼ pounds filet mignon, 1 inch thick, cut across the grain into 1-inch-wide by 2-inch-long slices

SAUCE

1 tablespoon oyster sauce

1½ teaspoons sesame oil

1½ teaspoons dark soy sauce

1½ teaspoons sugar

⅛ teaspoon white pepper

1 tablespoon cornstarch

¼ cup Chicken Stock (page 13)

PASTE

4 large cloves garlic, peeled and crushed

5 teaspoons fermented black beans, rinsed, drained

4 tablespoons peanut oil

1 slice ginger, ½ inch thick, peeled, lightly smashed

½ teaspoon salt

3 medium bell peppers, red, yellow, orange, or green, cut into 1-inch by 2-inch pieces

In a large bowl, mix marinade ingredients. Add beef, allow to rest at least 30 minutes. Reserve.

In a small bowl, mix sauce ingredients and reserve.

Mash garlic and black beans with handle of a cleaver and reserve.

Heat wok over high heat 30 seconds. Add 1½ tablespoons peanut oil, coat wok with spatula. When a wisp of white smoke appears, add ginger and salt, stir 40 seconds. Add peppers, stir together, cook for 1 minute. Turn off heat, transfer peppers to a bowl, reserve. Wipe off wok and spatula with paper towels.

Heat wok over high heat 30 seconds. Add remaining 2½ tablespoons peanut oil, coat wok with spatula. When a wisp of white smoke appears, add garlic–black bean paste, stir, cook until paste releases its fragrance, about 30 seconds. Add beef and marinade, spread in a thin layer. Cook for 1 to 2 minutes, tipping wok from side to side and turning beef once, to cook evenly. Add reserved peppers, stir-fry for 2 minutes. Make a well in the center of the mixture, stir sauce, pour in. Stir and cook, until sauce thickens and browns, 1 to 2 minutes. Transfer to a heated dish and serve immediately with cooked rice.

THIS DISH IS MEANT TO SERVE 6. IT RARELY DOES.

We have come to call this, in our family shorthand, Pepper Steak. Does it possess all the significance with which I invest it? I think it does.

All of our children ate Eileen's food from about six months of age—soft potatoes with a soupy meat-based sauce; steamed fish and rice; traditional rice congees. Never did she consider giving them prepared baby food—not even when I suggested that making it was an awful lot of trouble.

"For who?" she asked.

And there was the time I came home from work to find our apartment smelling as if it had been the venue for an all-day pot party. Not so. Eileen had smoked a duck in green tea. I told her she was lucky nobody called the police.

"They would have liked the duck," she suggested.

When I began writing in earnest about food and its traditions, first for the *New York Times*, later for *Gourmet* and other magazines, Eileen was my inspiration, my critic and my ultimate judge. Had I shown proper respect for the food and cooking about which I was writing? Had I written with precision? Had I tried to use fluid writing as a substitute for reporting and research? Had what I had written sounded like my voice? Her ear is perfect.

"Be sure to tell them that the roast chicken was deep-fried, not roasted," she cautioned, when I wrote of one Chinese meal we had eaten. "Get the spices right," she warned me. "I can't tell you how often tarragon is used but not mentioned by food critics."

For more than a quarter of a century, Eileen and I have had a Christmas Day feast—dining room table laden with Chinese food and accompanied by Champagne, only Champagne, which complements a range of her dishes beautifully. Eileen is the chef, I the sous chef, and we spend two weeks preparing pork, shrimp and vegetable dumplings; a tart Tianjin bok choy salad; broiled chunks of curried, honey-sweetened beef; cabbage and Thai chiles tossed in vinegar; shredded chicken in a sesame sauce; noodles with a crushed-peanut sauce clinging to them; stir-fried vegetables; rice; and a huge roasted fresh ham basted with soy sauce. The party is our Christmas gift to family and friends.

Over the years, I have suggested that Eileen was working too hard, preparing too many dishes. "This is for our friends," she would respond. "People we like. People we love."

End of argument.

—Fred Ferretti

INDEX

About the Author

Eileen Yin-Fei Lo is an educator and chef, and the author of nine previous cookbooks covering the breadth of Chinese cuisine. Born in a suburb of Canton, China, called Sun Tak, she began to cook at the age of five.

Ms. Lo is Consultant Chef at the China Institute in New York City, where she has taught cooking for more than twenty years. She also teaches Chinese cooking at the Culinary Arts Department of the New School University in New York.

In addition to her teaching and cookbooks, Ms. Lo has written on both food and restaurants for the *New York Times*, *New York Times Magazine*, *Gourmet*, *Food & Wine* and *Travel & Leisure*. She has consulted with various Four Seasons hotels and with many restaurants, including Shun Lee and Ruby Foo's in New York and Clio in Boston.

Ms. Lo is married to journalist and author Fred Ferretti. They live in Montclair, New Jersey, and have three children, Christopher, Elena and Stephen, and a granddaughter, Elliott Antonia.